SKH TO SKH
AND
EVOLUTIONARY GENESIS

SKH TO SKH
AND
EVOLUTIONARY GENESIS

An African-Centered Research Method

s³ḫw r s³ḫw (𓅮𓃀𓏤 — 𓅮𓃀𓏤)

WADE W. NOBLES, PHD

(Ifágbemì Sàngódáre)

"Our ontological and epistemolocal imperative is to
s³ḫw r s³ḫw, illuminate the illumined"

Nea Onnim
"When he who does not know learns, he gets to know."
Continued quest for knowledge.

SKH TO SKH
AND
EVOLUTIONARY GENESIS

An African-Centered Research Method

s³ḫw r s³ḫw (𓏃𓎱𓅱 ⸺ 𓏃𓎱𓅱)

Wade W. Nobles, PhD

(Ifágbemì Sàngódáre)

Little Black Book Series

RESEARCH METHODOLOGY, THEORY, AND PRAXIS

Volume 4

Universal Write Publications, LLC
New York, NY

SKH TO SKH AND EVOLUTIONARY GENESIS: AN AFRICAN-CENTERED
RESEARCH METHOD

Part of The Little Black Book Series

Library of Congress Control Number: 2025916354

PRINT: ISBN: 978-1-942774-54-9
eBOOK: ISBN: 978-1-942774-55-6
DOI: https://doi.org/10.65724/ZHHO9546

Printed in the United States of America.

Mailing/Submissions:

Universal Write Publications, LLC
421 8th avenue, Suite 86
New York, NY 10116

Website: www. uwpbooks.com

This publication was supported in part by a grant from Sage Publication.

Publisher's Cataloging-in-Publication Data

Nobels, Wade.
SKH TO SKH AND EVOLUTIONARY GENESIS: AN AFRICAN-CENTERED
RESEARCH METHOD / Dr. Wade Nobels. —
First Edition. — New York, NY: Universal Write Publications, 2025.
Includes bibliographical references.
Identifiers: LCCN 2025916354 | ISBN 978-1-942774-54-9 (pbk.) |
ISBN 978-1-942774-55-6 (ebook)
Subjects: LCSH Life histories—Research. | Qualitative methods—Africana Studies.

CLASSIFICATION: LCC GN345 .[C65] 2025 | DDC 300.72—dc23

Foreword

Necessary Epistemic and Paradigm Shifting

Skh to Skh: Evolutionary Genesis as an African-Centered Research Method is intentionally written, as the title explicitly states, to "illuminate the illumined." As a foreword and not a forward, I would like to emphasize the importance of "wording or langauging" in shifting the paradigm from western (White) thought to African-centered deep thought. This is essential and necessary for Africana research methodologists to understand and enhance the realities of African/Black people and to authentically and independently move ahead.

In introducing *Skh to Skh, Evolutionary Genesis and Divine Energy Made Manifest (DEMM)*, this text explores an African-centered ontological and epistemological paradigm that affirms the inherent spirit(ness), power, resilience, and connectivity of people of African ascent. In this work, Nobles challenges all expression of White thought, values, and beliefs vested in what is known as Westernization. The word *Skh* requires one to think deeply (illuminate) and profoundly about African meanings and understandings of the nature of being human. *Skh* is a process of understanding, examining, and explicating the meaning, nature, and functioning of being human for African people by conducting a deep, profound, and penetrating search, study, and mastery of the process of "illuminating" the human spirit and the totality of all human experiences and phenomena. *Skh (Djr)* operates from the basic premise that there is an African way of being that reflects an African "quality of thought and practice." Thusly, *Skh* is the word guiding the paradigm shifting in this contribution.

This book lays the foundations for the development of an authentic methodology that is grounded in, and consistent with, the African episteme. For too long, African-centered scholarship, research, and analysis have been crippled by the lack of an authentic methodology that is consistent with the emergence of authentic theoretical and conceptual formulation developed by the visionary, futuristic, and forward-thinking African-centered/ Black scholars. African-centered scholars, theoreticians, researchers who are engaging in paradigm shifting from the Eurocentric perspective have been stymied having to use methodological tools, techniques, and instruments that are inconsistent with the dictates of this shift. In short, African-centered researchers were engaged in conceptually incarcerated analysis that limited their ability to understand, explain the full range of the Black experience. That is, Eurocentric tools that are based on the individual and materialistic understanding of being human are conceptually and structurally incapable of measuring the synergistic entity of the Black experience.

In shifting the paradigm, Nobles has opened up a portal for a more attuned methodological approach to African-centered research. The challenge for the Black researchers is to ask new and different questions of the Black experience while at the same time assessing, refining, and expanding the methodological framework provided by Nobles for the rescue, reclamation, and restoration of the African way of being.

This contribution provides, describes, explains, and illustrates the African-centered paradigm shifting necessary for Africana research methodologists to understand and enhance the realities of African/ Black people. It is consistent with the mission and purpose of the *Little Black Book Series* as it offers a culturally congruent

(African-centered) research praxis for humanizing, life-affirming, and liberatory methodologies essential to Africana Studies. This text will free the researcher from the prism of western research modalities and help the Africana researcher to understand, but more importantly implement, research methodologies specifically designed to explore, enhance, explain, describe, and advance African/Black communities.

Lawford L. Goddard, PhD

Association of Black Psychologists

ABPsi

Western Region

Contents

Introduction

s³ḥw r s³ḥw (𓄖𓏤 ⸗ 𓄖𓏤) *Skh to Skh: Evolutionary Genesis as an African-Centered Research Method* represents the third iteration of the Skh. The first, *Seeking the Sakhu: Foundational Writings for an African Psychology* (2006) provided the first introduction to the idea of "illumination" as a guiding theme in the evolution of African (Black) psychology. *Seeking the Sakhu ...* called for us to more than merely dismantle the ideological, behavioral, and physical structures of domination, but to repair that which has been in ruins and knit ourselves back together again. The second iteration, *Skh, From Black Psychology to the Science of Being* (2023) represents a bold shift in Black psychology's evolution from discipline to a science of being. With hindsight, it was written to allow the reader to "wade in the ancient Nile' river of thought," "shower with the cool waters of traditional BaNtu peoples," and "sun bathe in African ascendency" as a mysterious scaffolding mind-scaping walk in the sun of illumination. There is a connection between science and technology, and, within technology, there is methodology.

This book, *s³ḥw r s³ḥw* (𓄖𓏤 ⸗ 𓄖𓏤) *Skh to Skh and Evolutionary Genesis Research Methodology through African Eyes*, the third in the Skh trilogy, explores my quest for intellectual illumination that clarified, named, and married my long journey to the idea of "evolutionary genesis as a foundational research methodology within SKH (the Science of Being) which reflects a paradigmatic African-centered framework that investigates the nature and purpose of human existence."

We, Black psychologists, need to divorce ourselves from White psychology and establish sole custody, and giving no visitation rights nor requests for child support regarding Black mental health. By extension, this decree should also include all expressions of White thought, values, and beliefs vested in what is known as Westernization. We and our work will have no value to African-ascended people as long as we are trapped in the conceptual incarcerated approaches to understanding African life and living (Nobles, 1978). Conceptual incarceration underscores the fundamental necessity of critically examining and, where necessary, rejecting externally imposed conceptual frameworks in favor of those who genuinely reflect the lived realities and cultural contexts of African peoples. Accordingly, in retrospect and as a preemptory prescription for all future contributions, all intellectual, activists, knowledge production, and programmatic contributions, should be filtered through the intentional attempts and desire to take the authority to unapologetically and uncompromisingly embrace, establish, and honor paradigmatic shifting and praxis.

Word/concepts are instruments of languaging that describe/define phenomena or aspect thereof that locate (hold) an idea(s) in space, time, and place. The word serves to identify, explain, and understand. Words, it seems to me, are tools for "meaning-making." As meaning-making tools, words or concepts assist in our understanding and/or explaining the phenomena in question being identified. The acts of knowing and being and the words selected to guide the process are filtered through the agency of culture, worldview, episteme, paradigm, and narrative. It is culture as represented in narrative that looms critical.

The Western Grand Narrative is the overarching historical story that Europe and its settler offshoots (e.g., the United States) have told about themselves for centuries to the "rest of us." This narrative rationalizes and justifies conquest, enslavement, and extermination by defining indigenous Black peoples as less-than-human, savage, or needing civilization (African Colonization). It celebrates the extraction of resources, labor, and capital from the non-White world as evidence of divine favor and personal merit (avaricious accumulation and hoarding of wealth). White psychology operationalizes and refines the Western Grand narrative as "scientific" and by so doing functions as a legitimizing arm of the Western Grand Narrative by defining Eurocentric norms as universal. Euro-American (White) psychology establishes White, Western cultural norms—independence, linear logic, nuclear family structure, competition—as universal standards of mental health and human development, reducing human complexity (gender, age, race, caste/class) to separate features that can be observed, categorized, and manipulated. The White psychology is the legitimizing arm of the Western Grand Narrative. It elevates the idea that individualism and individuals are self-contained, autonomous, and solely responsible for their outcomes ("rugged individualism").

This clinical gaze generated by White psychology pathologizes Blackness and sees Blackness as deviancy. Euro-American psychology did not simply "reflect" anti-Blackness, it produced, codified, and weaponized it under the guise of objective science. Euro-American (White) psychology forged the ideological blueprints that continue to justify Blackness as other and in need of domination, exploitation, oppression, and even elimination. The Western (white) grand narrative gives primacy to the itemization, separateness, and individualism of "entity" over essence, expression, and experience. Euro-American (White) psychology forged the ideological research blueprint.

In the paradigm shifting reflected in *Skh to Skh and Evolutionary Genesis, Research Methodology through African Eyes,* we have attempted to assert an African-centered narrative that supports the interconnected rings of personhood, familyhood, and neighborhood, which purports that wellness, both as a personal state and a collective goal, can be envisioned as a series of concentric rings, each representing a different level of human interconnectedness. The three rings consist of **personhood**, which exists within **familyhood** that is embedded in **neighborhood** (community). "Personhood" is the special, unique or distinct, personal attributes, characteristics, and qualities that are particular manifestations of the community (whole). "Familyhood" consists of those yet-to-be-born, the living, and those in the afterlife. "Neighborhood" (community) is the identifiable area defined by particular historical experiences, worldview, value system, social institutions, and traditions. The three concentric rings, personhood, familyhood, and neighborhood, are dynamically linked. Each ring influences and bolsters the others.

The linkage between the Interconnecting Rings of Personhood, Familyhood, and Neighborhood model has three key energetic concepts, *Zola, Ngolo, and Kinsukami* that serve as catalysts for vitalism, interconnectedness, and regeneration, respectively. *Zola*, understood as love, *Ngolo*, as healing capacity to thrive, and *Kinsukami* as dignity that is tied to one's vitality, value, self-worth, moral standing and ancestral alignment. Dignity affirms that a person walks in harmony with the divine and reflects *Zola* (love) and *Ngolo* as complementary energetic forces that animate and sustain wellness and vitality.

Ultimately, words and languaging are tools for "meaning-making." As meaning-making tools, words or concepts assist in paradigmatic framing for researching the understanding and/or explaining the phenomena in question being identified. The act of knowing and being and the words selected to guide the process are filtered through the agency of culture, worldview, episteme paradigm, and narrative. It is culture as reflected through narrative and paradigm that guides all research, and it is *Skh to Skh and Evolutionary Genesis* that is being offered as essential.

Overview: Chapter 1 introduces the intellectual and philosophical grounding for the Skh to Skh and evolutionary genesis. Chapter 2 explores the idea of "*evolutionary genesis*" as a new paradigm for engaging in African-centered research. Chapter 3 discusses being spirit beings. Chapter 4 explains how being spirit(ness) is the heart of African-centered Research. Chapter 5 directly explores the full or whole African reality as both visible and invisible realms of reality and the complete domain for researching life and living. Chapter 6 gives an exposition of a research paradigm for understanding being spirit as the evolutionary genesis approach, and Chapter 7 introduces a new research program for understanding being spirit. Chapter 8 exposes the research methodologists with a preliminary rethinking of the African (BaNtu) question of insanity, critical to African-centered research. Chapter 9 challenges the African-centered methodologist to see research not just as a tool for knowing and validating real(ity) but to affirm Being and being "mo betta." Chapter 10 provides a summary and implications for Africana research designed to "illuminate the Illumined" (Sakhu to Sakhu) through evolutionary genesis that reflects an evolving research methodology for Africana and Africology rooted in ancestral memory, spirit, and sovereignty. The final Chapter 11 ponders possible next steps. In so doing, this book reflects and directs the future intellectual heritage of Africana and Africology scholars to be marked by what I have identified as paradigm shifting, illumination, and evolutionary genesis.

Each chapter is written as an invitation to Africana research methodologist to ponder, explore, and be stimulated by the possibilities that emerge from "paradigm shifting" and seeing knowledge production with or through African eyes.

CHAPTER 1
New Groundings

The grounding for **Sakhu to Sakhu and Evolutionary genesis** as an exploratory congruent African-centered research methodology is found in Ancient Kemet and Traditional BaNtu thought. In Kemetic philosophy, Sakhu *sꜣḫw* (𓐍𓏭𓄿) means "sacred illumination and the luminous being." It refers to a spirit-defined awakened or "transfigured" being. It is both a noun and a verb, both a *state of being* and *process of becoming*. Sakhu sꜣḫw 𓐍𓏭𓄿 expresses the concept of *spirit-soul-light* or *intellectual/spiritual illumination*. Sakhu (sꜣḫw) is often translated as the "spirit-intellect," "illuminated consciousness."

In Kemetic cosmology, the root sꜣḫw (sakhu or sakhu) refers to the *spiritual body* or *the illuminated aspect of being*, which survives physical death and ascends to realms of higher consciousness. The phrase "sꜣḫw r sꜣḫw" therefore refers not simply to acquiring information, but to enhancing the luminosity of one's spirit-defined essence, a process deeply tied to ethical conduct (Ma'at), ancestral continuity, and divine order. Rather than a linear trajectory, Kemetic illumination is cyclical and spiraled.

The ancient Kemetic phrase sᵇḫw r sᵇḫw (𓈖𓏤 — 𓈖𓏤), often transliterated as "to illuminate the illumined" or "to cause the enlightened to become more enlightened," encapsulates a fundamental African epistemological principle: knowledge, consciousness, and being are not static states but dynamic, spiraling processes of continual becoming. To "illuminate the illumined" means to go deeper into wisdom one already holds, to refine light with more light, and to harmonize one's essence with cosmic order (tᵇ ntr—divine speech/logic). It suggests a pedagogy and cosmology of eternal unfolding, where being is not an endpoint but a movement toward higher frequencies of existence. Sakhu sᵇḫw 𓈖𓏤 reflects an ontological consciousness that is not static but luminous, eternal, and ethical, a being who has become one with Ma'at, divine order, truth, reciprocity, and cosmic harmony (Nobles, 2006, p. 57).

It means "to cause to become sᵇḫw for the sake of becoming sᵇḫw," an unfolding process of transforming into one who is spiritually awakened or spiritually luminous. This ancient concept conveys a recursive, initiatory process of becoming—of "becoming the one who becomes," aligning with the Kemetic ideal of eternal becoming (nfr) and sacred continuity. It captures both the cosmological and epistemological rhythm of life as understood in African antiquity: a spiraling journey of return, refinement, illumination, and return.

The phrase sᵇḫw r sᵇḫw (𓈖𓏤 — 𓈖𓏤) to become sᵇḫw in order to become sᵇḫw indicates a recursive sacred process. It mirrors the African metaphysical notion that life is an initiatory journey in which one must repeatedly refine the self to become increasingly attuned to divine principles. Dr Jacob Carruthers (1999) writes that the process of *becoming* in African cosmology is a spiraling return, a dialectic of remembrance and transformation, deeply rooted in moral character and ancestral consciousness.

s²ḥw r s²ḥw is an ontological and epistemological imperative. It symbolizes the African journey of eternal becoming, of spiraling return, and of sacred restoration. The phrase s²ḥw r s²ḥw harmonizes with Evolutionary genesis as a model of African-centeredness. This principle finds full expression in the contemporary concept of evolutionary genesis, which frames knowledge generation and human development as an ongoing reclamation, refinement, and reconstitution of ancestral wisdom as the basis for future becoming. It represents illumination as "continuous becoming," a spiritual-philosophical movement from divine knowing to divine knowing, or being illuminating being. It is both conceptually profound and spiritually recursive. It reflects the cyclical and regenerative nature of divine illumination and wisdom transmission.

Evolutionary genesis reactivates the imperative in our time, enabling African-ascended peoples to reenter the cosmic flow of meaning, dignity, and divine energy. The contemporary framework of evolutionary genesis aligns with this ancient Kemetic concept.

The Bantu–Kongo believe that the heated force of Kalunga blew up and down as a huge storm of projectiles, *kimbwandende*, fusing together a huge mass. In the process of cooling, solidification of the fused mass occurs, giving birth to the Earth (Fu-Kiau, 2001). In effect, the Bantu believe that all of reality (*kalunga*) is fundamentally a process of perpetual and mutual sending and receiving of spirit (energy) in the form of waves and radiations. *Kalunga* or reality is the totality, the completeness of all life. It is an ocean of energy, a force in motion. *Kalunga* is everything, sharing life and becoming life continually after life itself. As the totality or the complete living, *kalunga* is comprised of both a visible realm (*ku nseke*) and an invisible realm (*ku mpemba*). The visible physical world has spirit (energy) as its most important element or nature. Referred to as *nkisi* (medicine), the spirit element of the physical (visible) world has the power to care, cure, heal, and guide. The invisible (spirit-defined) world (*ku mpemba*) is comprised of human experience, ancestor experience, and the soul–mind experience. The *ku mpemba* has spirit (energy) as its most important element or nature. In effect, if reality (visible and invisible) is, it is spirit. All that exists are, therefore, different concrete expressions of spirit. In effect, "Being" is being spirit in a reality of spirit. Fu-Kiau (2001) further clarifies that the human being or *muntu* is a "threefold unfolding" experience in the realms of yet-to-live, living, and after-living. He further notes that a human being is a living sun (energy), possessing "knowing and knowable" spirit (energy) through which spirit in human form has an enduring relationship with the total perceptible and ponderable universe. The Bantu–Kongo believe that diverse forces and waves of energy govern life surrounding humans. This fire force called *kalunga* is complete in and of itself and emerges within the emptiness or nothingness and becomes the source of life on earth (see Dikenga chart below).

Accordingly, in the BaNtu world, real(ity) (*Kalunga*) is fundamentally a process of perpetual and mutual sending and receiving of spirit (energy) in the form of waves and radiations. The material universe is only the perception of real(ity), that is, in fact, non-localized, immutable, and eternal spirit. What is real(ity) (*Kalunga*) is comprised of both a visible realm (*Ku Nseke, Aye*) and an invisible realm (*Ku Mpemba, Orun*). The visible realm is considered the "microcosmos," the immediate perceptible world. The invisible realm is considered the "mesocosmos," the intermediate world of spirits, genies, and beneficial/malevolent forces. The "macrocosmos," the world beyond the senses, the realm of the Divine, ancestors, and spirit beings. Reality consists of the visible and the invisible with the invisible being far greater than the visible.

Kongo for moments of the Sun

Dikenga
Kongo Cosmos
(Four Moments of the Sun)

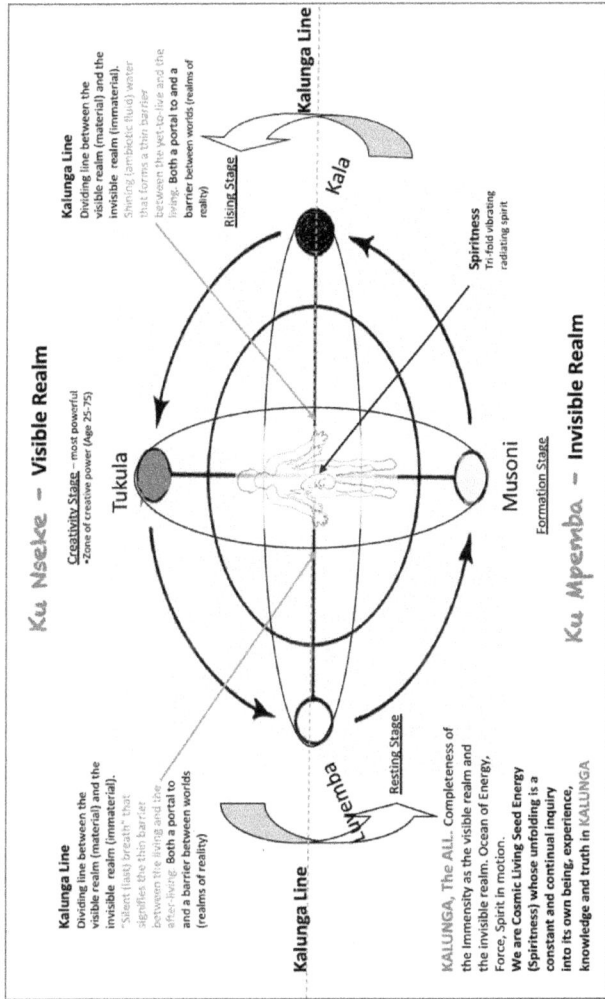

Ku Nseke – Visible Realm

Ku Mpemba – Invisible Realm

Tukula

Kala

Musoni

Luvemba

Creativity Stage – most powerful
•Zone of creative power (Age 25-75)

Rising Stage

Formation Stage

Resting Stage

Kalunga Line
Dividing line between the visible realm (material) and the invisible realm (immaterial). Shining (symbiotic fluid) water that forms a thin barrier between the yet-to-live and the living. Both a portal to and a barrier between worlds (realms of reality)

Kalunga Line
Dividing line between the visible realm (material) and the invisible realm (immaterial). "Silent (last) breath" that signifies the thin barrier between the living and the after-living. Both a portal to and a barrier between worlds (realms of reality)

Kalunga Line

Spiritness
Tri-fold vibrating radiating spirit

KALUNGA, The ALL. Completeness of the Immensity as the visible realm and the invisible realm. Ocean of Energy, Force, Spirit in motion.
We are Cosmic Living Seed Energy (Spiritness) whose unfolding is a constant and continual inquiry into its own being, experience, knowledge and truth in KALUNGA

Nobles, W.W. (2009-12) augmentation in collaboration with Kimwandende Kia Bunseke Fu-Kiau *Simba Simbi: A Deep insight Retreat Into Traditional African Systems of Health and Healing* (also see, *Tying the Spiritual Knot: African Cosmology of the Bantu-Kongo*)

All that exists are, therefore, different concrete expressions of spirit (*Ntu*).

African deep thought and wisdom traditions suggest that the universe is "matter" in appearance, and "spirit" in reality. The material universe is only the perception of reality, that is, in fact, non-localized, immutable, and eternal spirit. African epistemology, consequently, imprints the natural centrality of the role of the Divine and of the "Spirit" in the acquisition of knowledge (Advice V. & Pascha Mungwini, 2010). Based in the interrogation of the knowing implications of classical civilizations of Kmt (Egypt) and Nubia, the ancient beliefs of the Bantu and Kongo people (Nobles, 2015b) proposed that an African grand narrative be called *Kmt-Nubian—Bantu/Kongo*. The African grand narrative, *Kmt- Nubian—Bantu/Kongo*, in turn, understands that all in reality is "Spirit" or "Energy" and that a particular process of knowing emerges from African genesis or creation myths, the meaning of being human, and the concept of life and death.

Using indigenous epistemic reflections, cultural appreciations, and apperceptions about reality to inform their knowing framework and intellectual mindset, the African Grand Narrative as the mindset for guiding counseling, treatment, and research would be a constructive process, reflecting deep intrinsic African beliefs as both descriptive and explanatory discourse by which Africans interpret and reinterpret their experiences in order to recognize, record, and make sense of events and experiences, especially knowing and knowledge production. The power of the grand narrative is that it shapes and influences what we see and accept as normal. The African grand narrative shapes and influences, without European or Western interference, what is understood to be and accepted as normal.

All humans use their own epistemic reflections, cultural appreciations, and apperceptions about reality to inform how they "know" and "think," which, in turn, allows one to further recognize and record events and experiences as well as "make sense" out of reality. It defines and determines (1) how reality is defined through an African episteme (knowing/understanding); (2) the nature of reality; (3) how truth is determined; (4) that which is knowable and can be known; and (5) what the relationship is between knowing (process); the known (subject) and the knower (being)—what should/could be done in response to the known.

The so-called BaNtu expansion is believed to have first originated around the Benue–Cross Rivers area in Southeastern Nigeria and spread over Africa to the Zambia area. Sometime in the second millennium BC, the BaNtu were forced to expand into the rainforest of Central Africa. Later, the BaNtu began a more rapid second phase of expansion beyond the forests into Southern and Eastern Africa reaching modern day Zimbabwe and South Africa. Another theory held that the BaNtu originated from the Congo and spread out to the north, east, and the south. Whether going from north to south or south to north, it should be clear that the BaNtu spread out over most of Africa and with the experience of the slave trade spread equally throughout the new world. The primary evidence for this great expansion (Ehret, 2001), one of the largest in human history, has been linguistic, namely, that the languages spoken in sub-Equatorial Africa are remarkably similar to one other, to the degree that it is unlikely that they began diverging from each other more than 3,000 years ago. The BaNtu people with their culture, language, family, spirit-defined beliefs, and philosophical ideas are the very people stolen and kidnapped in the Transatlantic slave trade. In effect, BaNtu beliefs and ideas were embedded in the various peoples who were stolen and kidnapped.

Africans on the continent and throughout the diaspora are fundamentally BaNtu people. In fact, it is only in understanding the

BaNtu–Kongo ideas and meanings of being human that one will be able to better or more fully determine the impact of the Trans-Saharan and Transatlantic slave trade. In terms of beliefs and African deep thought, Ngubane (1979) argued that the African understanding of the person is a "protein" evaluation of the human being, which flowed into Nile Valley high culture of the Ancient Kemites and subsequently created clusters of similar conceptions all over Africa. What, in fact, is recognized as African American culture is the combined social conventions and inventions emerging from a common African root meaning of the person.

Throughout African cosmological traditions, communication extends beyond speech, gestures, or written symbols, encompassing vibrational frequencies, energetic transmissions, and metaphysical resonances that bind the seen and unseen realms. Among the BaNtu, knowledge is neither passive nor static but a dynamic interplay of forces, energies, and harmonized relationships facilitating the continuous transference of wisdom. This understanding provides a foundational basis for what may be termed bio-phonic communication—the transference of energetic information across realms through vibrational frequencies, sound waves, and bioenergetic signatures. The BaNtu epistemic frame perceives knowledge as living and sound as a carrier of being, intention, and transformation, aligning with notions of interconnectedness, spirit, and collective knowing.

Bioenergetic signature: Bioenergetic signature refers to the unique vibrational, spirit-defined, and energetic imprint that a being—whether human, ancestral, or divine—carries and transmits. This signature consists of distinct frequencies, rhythms, and resonance patterns that encode one's essence, personality, spirit-defined attributes, and intergenerational memory. In BaNtu epistemology, these signatures are foundational in bio-phonic communication, ensuring that ancestral and spirit-defined messages are recognizable, traceable, and coherent across realms.

Zaya as a Bioenergetic Signature: *Zaya (v) is a KiKongo* term meaning to know, to imagine. Zaya represents the reemergence, continuity, and re-manifestation of an ancestor's essence within a descendant. It is an energetic signature that functions as an ancestral echo wave, ensuring that the life force (mpeve) of an ancestor remains active across generations. This ancient term was rescued, expanded, and reinterpreted as "Zaya Discourse," meaning the ability to remember and imagine additional authentic culturally congruent (African-centered) thoughts, ideas, and knowing stimulated by communal conversation. Zaya helps reveal what was lost or distorted as well as assists in creating "signposts" (Imagination and memory) for reclaiming our way and restoring wellness going forward. "Zaya Discourse" depends on "memory" (engaging realms of reality and identifying, recalling, and rescuing ideas, beliefs, values, customs, and experiences) and "imagination" (cocreating wonderment around new and refined ideas, beliefs, behaviors, values, customs, activities, and experiences). The Zaya Discourse Process is an openly and unapologetically culturally congruent (African-centered) initiative designed in alignment with African and African ancestry cultural reality and Skh Tm (advanced Pan-African Black psychology).

As a unique vibrational imprint, *zaya* expresses itself in multiple ways: (1) Physical and Behavioral Reincarnation (*Kutumbula*), wherein a descendant may inherit physical features, mannerisms, speech patterns, or distinctive habits of a deceased elder, even without direct exposure to them. This energetic encoding ensures that the presence of the ancestor persists in a new form; (2) Spontaneous Recall and Memory Activation, wherein individuals with *zaya* may experience unexplained knowledge or memory flashes related to ancestral experiences, locations, or wisdom, without having learned them in the material sense. This aligns with the concept of genetic and ancestral memory, (3) Inherited spirit-defined or artistic talents, wherein a child may display musical, storytelling, healing, or artistic skills identical to those of a known ancestor. This is seen in the transmission of griot traditions, spirit-defined leadership, and artistic mastery, (4) Dream Messages and Astral Visitations, wherein Individuals carrying *zaya* may receive direct communication from the ancestor whose energy they embody, appearing in dreams or trance states to offer guidance, warnings, or affirmations; (5) Restoring (Healing) and Protective Energies, wherein certain descendants may inherit ancestral healing abilities, manifesting as intuitive knowledge of herbal medicine, spirit-defined rituals, and energy work; and (6) Manifestation in Synchronized Life Events, whereby *Zaya* can also express itself through life paths mirroring those of ancestors, such as career choices, personal struggles, and even relationships that seem to follow a predestined ancestral pattern.

Ngolo the kinetic force: In BaNtu cosmology, Ngolo represents spirit-defined strength, resilience, and the ability to channel divine energy into action. It is a force that drives motion, transformation, and power. *Zaya* does not simply exist—it is activated and propelled by Ngolo, ensuring that ancestral memory, inherited talents, and spirit-defined callings are expressed dynamically in the physical world.

The ways Ngolo expresses *Zaya* are as (1) the spirit-defined energy behind inherited talents. Herein *Zaya* manifests artistic, musical, and healing talents, but Ngolo is what energizes these abilities, allowing them to flourish. This is why certain individuals experience sudden awakenings or skill enhancements when their Ngolo is elevated; (2) the bio-phonic conduit for ancestral communication. When ancestors communicate, their messages are carried through Ngolo-driven frequencies, ensuring that individual's *zaya* can receive guidance and insight. Drumming, chanting, and spirit-defined movement (dance) enhances Ngolo, making communication more precise and powerful; (3) the strengthening of *Zaya* through movement. Ritual movements, such as Capoeira or Engolo (a warrior dance from Angola), are manifestations of Ngolo reinforcing *Zaya*. Many warriors inherit their ancestors' combative instincts, reflexes, and strategies, expressed through Ngolo-powered motion; and (4) protection and healing power. Healers use Ngolo to amplify their *zaya*-inherited gifts, allowing them to channel living light in healing rituals. Individuals with strong Ngolo often display spirit-defined resilience, warding off negative energies while attracting ancestral support.

In the BaNtu cosmological framework, "living light" is the vibrational essence of ancestral presence, existing as an intelligent and dynamic energy field that transcends physical limitations. This light serves as a carrier of *zaya*, reinforcing the continuity of life and knowledge across generations. Living Light operates through coherent energy fields, much like bio-photons in quantum physics, which transmit information nonlocally.

Paradigm shifting: In building on the relational aspect of African worldviews, I have proposed a model of interconnecting rings personhood, familyhood, and neighborhood (peoplehood) to represent experience where personhood, familyhood, and neighborhood/peoplehood stand as expressions of the features of being spirit.

In African-centered thought, human identity and wellness are neither individualistic nor isolated phenomena. Rather, they emerge from a deeply relational cosmology where the self (personhood), the family, and the surrounding community (neighborhood) exist in sacred interconnection. These three spheres form what can be described as interconnecting rings of personhood, familyhood, and neighborhood/peoplehood with wellness residing at their overlapping core. This indigenous construct challenges Eurocentric paradigms that prioritize autonomous individualism and instead affirms a communal ontology wherein being is grounded in "inter-being" or relationship (Nobles, 2006, p. 45).

The African-centered model of interconnecting rings of personhood, familyhood, and neighborhood with wellness at the center affirms that well-being is communal, spirit-defined, and dynamic. It is a state of harmonious entanglement, echoing quantum notions of coherence, where being and belonging interweave. Restoration of wellness, then, is the sacred task of reconnecting the dismembered self to the ancestral and communal whole, affirming one's Divine Energy Made Manifest (DEMM) within the shared rhythms of life.

This framework is rooted in African-centered episteme where knowledge is gained through experiential, relational, and spirit-defined dimensions. It focuses on embodied knowledge, community wisdom, and ancestral teachings as integral to understanding wellness. The research process in this framework is often participatory, communal, and restorative. In the interconnecting rings framework, the context is crucial. The human experience is never individually isolated but must be viewed within the context of relationships (family, community, ancestors, environment). It integrates the visible and invisible realms (e.g., physical health and ancestral spiritual wellness) and how the visible and invisible are seamless. This framework would promote research that considers how intergenerational trauma or ancestral disconnection, for instance, can influence present-day wellness, providing a multidimensional view of human experience. The concept of interconnecting rings with wellness at their overlapping core presents a holistic and relational framework for understanding being as personhood, familyhood, and neighborhood (peoplehood). This approach differs significantly from traditional group cohort studies that typically focus on statistical analysis within isolated variables, often without incorporating the deeper interconnectedness and the multidimensional, contextual understanding of well-being. The interconnecting rings framework highlights epigenetics, intergenerational vision, and historical memory as crucial aspects of wellness. Research in this area would explore how ancestral experiences of colonization, slavery, and forced migration impact present-day health and identity. This shift could lead to new investigations into how ancestral memory and spiritual practices impact individual and collective resilience, shaping how communities respond to collective trauma.

The interconnecting rings framework invites the Africana research methodologists to challenge traditional research paradigms by emphasizing interconnectedness, relationality, and a holistic understanding of wellness. It encourages research that integrates African-centered epistemologies, community engagement, and spirituality, broadening the scope of inquiry beyond isolated variables to embrace the multidimensional and intergenerational aspects of human experience.

Ultimately, to frame research is to make a declaration about the nature of reality, the purpose of inquiry, and the pathway toward truth. The Western notion of "nomological-deductive reasoning" offers a framework of logic and law suited for prediction and control, but often disconnected from the cultural, spiritual, and communal life worlds of African people. The interconnecting rings of personhood, familyhood, and neighborhood/peoplehood offer a paradigm rooted in African ways of being and knowing—one that views research not merely as knowledge production, but as an act of healing, coherence, and spiritual alignment. It invites researchers not to stand outside of life, seeking to explain it, but to stand within it, seeking to restore the sacred web of Being.

The paradigm shifting required by the proposed exploratory African-centered congruent research methodology creates a special challenge for the Africana researcher. Very little work has been done outside of the western materialistic realm and individualistic framework. What is being offered in this contribution is a radical shift in the knowing and knowledge production enterprise.

The implications of this contrast are profound. When framed through the "nomological-deductive reasoning" model, research tends to abstract from lived experience in order to find generalizable patterns. Such knowledge may be statistically significant but "existentially shallow," especially when applied to African-descended communities whose realities are shaped by spiritual, historical, and communal dimensions often invisible to empirical positivism.

By contrast, the interconnected rings of personhood, familyhood, and neighborhood/peoplehood framework insists that research must begin with spirit-defined intentions, culturally rooted questions, and healing-centered outcomes. It emphasizes ethical embeddedness, ancestral responsibility, and intergenerational accountability. It reframes what counts as evidence, how it is interpreted, and for whom it is meaningful. It does not aim to predict outcomes across contexts but to reharmonize lives within context.

Accordingly, all the elements of the research enterprise, that is, population sampling, hypotheses generation/testing, analyses, results interpretation, will need to be revisited, and the Africana research methodologist/theorist should be given license to create and/or invent culturally congruent (African-centered) and epistemically coherent ideas, concepts, and procedures.

The discussion in the following chapters is inspired by African deep thought (worldview) and the requisite paradigm shifting to spirit being (DEMM) and the African-centered model of interconnecting rings of personhood, familyhood, and neighborhood/peoplehood with wellness at the center.

CHAPTER 2
sᵌḥw r sᵌḥw and Evolutionary Genesis

This chapter explores the definitions, functions, and paradigm shifting implications of *sᵌḥw r sᵌḥw* and evolutionary genesis as groundbreaking contributions to the Science of Being, particularly within the Africana world. Across time and terrain, human civilizations have sought to answer the enduring questions: *Who are we? What is the nature of our existence? How do we come to know ourselves and others?* In Western traditions, these inquiries have often been fragmented, dividing the self from the soul, spirit-defined from the scientific. Earlier. I suggested that Black Studies, was a "vitalistic synergetic multidimensional science" grounded in an African philosophical world view and epistemology. As such, Black Studies should be compelled to explore the complete contours (contexts, contents, and conditions) of the African notion of human "essence" or spirit (Nobles, 2019). *Skh, From Black Psychology to the Science of Being* is offered as an integrative vision of being as spirit and understanding not as an abstraction but as a living force encoded in the cosmos, the land, the community, and the self.

As noted, the Kemetic declaration *sꜣḫw r sꜣḫw* is not a redundant utterance, but a profound reminder that illumination is never complete only deepened. It urges us to approach knowledge, identity, and spirit as living energies that must be continually cultivated. Evolutionary genesis offers a 21st-century framework to enact this principle, empowering African peoples to rescue, refine, and regenerate their genius as a spirit-defined and scientific imperative. In doing so, we honor the sacred charge to *illuminate the illumined* and fulfill the highest mandate of African-centered being: to become more divine, more luminous, more whole. In all areas, evolutionary genesis operationalizes *sꜣḫw r sꜣḫw* as both a spirit obligation and methodological commitment to develop from within our own illuminated blueprint.

The concept of "evolutionary genesis," as proposed, offers a nuanced approach to knowledge acquisition and epistemological reflection that are deeply rooted in African intellectual traditions. It represents *"The evolutionary process of rescuing, reclaiming, and refining ancient African thought, ideas, epistemic reflections, philosophy, wisdom, and intellectual traditions as genesis for guiding the ongoing organic development and unfolding of concepts, constructs, methods, theories, programs, research and services,"* while positioning it as a *genesis*, or foundational principle, for the ongoing organic development of contemporary thought, constructs, and applied methodologies. The term *genesis*, enriched with the prefix "gen," not only alludes to beginnings but emphasizes genetic, gene, genome, generation, genuineness, genesis, all of which support the innate potential for new development in areas of intellectual inquiry and practical implementation.

Evolutionary genesis mirrors or manages *sꜣḫw r sꜣḫw* in the following critical ways: (1) **Rescue and Return:** Evolutionary genesis involves returning to the source, the cultural and spiritual archives of African antiquity to reclaim what was distorted, lost, or suppressed. This is akin to *sᶦḥw* as the act of becoming luminous through remembering one's essence. (2) **Refinement and Rebirth:** In becoming *sᶦḥw*, one is not merely recalling but refining, elevating, and radiating divine consciousness. Evolutionary genesis emphasizes this same process by refining epistemological tools that birth liberatory paradigms. (3) **Continuity Across Realms:** Both concepts emphasize being and becoming across realms (visible and invisible), physical and metaphysical, a crucial African epistemological hallmark (see Fu-Kiau, 2001).

Thus, "evolutionary genesis," is the *methodological embodiment* of *sᶦḥw r sᶦḥw*. It is how African knowledge becomes radiant again in contemporary form, through ancestral resonance and cosmological integrity. Together, *sᶦḥw r sᶦḥw* and evolutionary genesis form a transhistorical bridge uniting ancestral brilliance with present-day reawakening and future radiance with direct relevance to liberatory African psychology. This union reveals that becoming *sᶦḥw* is both our ancestral calling and our evolutionary destiny.

In *SKH, From Black Psychology to the Science of Being* (Nobles, 2023), African-centered psychology must move beyond "being human" to "being Spirit." This notion of *Spirit(ness)* that we are spirit beings housed in physical containers reclaims our original nature as luminous energy (*DEMM*). To become *sᶦḥw* is to become DEMM in form. The recursive phrase *sᶦḥw r sᶦḥw* embodies this ontological return to our true, radiant being. Similarly, "evolutionary genesis," provides the epistemic framework through which we reconstruct this luminous beingness as an analytic, therapeutic, and cultural imperative. This also resonates with the scientific metaphor of quantum entanglement. Just as particles separated by space are still deeply connected, African beings are entangled across temporal, ancestral, and cosmological planes. To "become again what we were" (Carruthers, 1999, p. 77) is not metaphorical but quantum in effect evoking the principles of bio-phonic communication, noetic sensoria, and ancestral memory.

Evolutionary genesis is therefore an African-centered methodological and epistemological paradigm defined as the process of rescuing, reclaiming, refining, and regenerating ancestral African thought and spiritual wisdom as the genesis (beginning point) for new development and becoming. It recognizes African wisdom traditions as living, organic repositories that are not to be mimicked as fixed traditions, but engaged as catalytic codes for evolutionary forward-motion. As an epistemic model, "evolutionary genesis" grounds knowledge in ancestral memory and cosmological alignment; views knowledge production as a spirit-defined act; operates within both the visible and invisible realms of reality; and treats time as spiral, not linear, prioritizing remembrance and innovation. It emphasizes that authentic growth is not from adopting alien paradigms, but from evolving out of one's deepest ancestral truths, the wisdom and light already embedded within

The relationship between *sᶦḫw r sᶦḫw* and evolutionary genesis is one of deep philosophical and spiritual correspondence that *illuminates the illumined* and engages in evolutionary genesis. It recognizes that ancestral truths are already embedded in our being, and to bring those truths into higher resonance through conscious practice, refinement, and transmission.

At the heart of evolutionary genesis lies the process of *rescuing* ancient African thought from the recesses of colonization, historical erasure, and intellectual distortion. Grounded in the cosmological concept that humans are DEMM, African research methodology through African Eyes should extend beyond Western materialist paradigms to encompass visible and invisible realms of reality. The concept of *evolutionary genesis* lies in its capacity to generate frameworks that are not only culturally congruent but also intellectually robust. In defining DEMM as the population under study, the methodological framework articulates the relevance of *evolutionary genesis* as a new revolutionary research paradigm for investigating both visible and invisible African reality.

This exploratory discourse stands on the edge of the precipice of illumination and provides a platform for reaching beyond traditional thought. It defends the idea that ancestral memory, astral resonance, and spirit attunement are legitimate and measurable domains of study when operating within an African-centered cosmology. It concludes with a step-by-step procedure for implementing the concept of *evolutionary genesis* as a knowledge acquisition and development process followed by thought, stimulating procedures for sample selection, hypothesis generation, data analysis, etc., where African-centered research methodology supports the restoration of wellness and alignment within and across realms for African ascendant people.

The foundational notion, Skh Djr,[1] requires one to think deeply and profoundly about African meanings and understandings of the nature of being human. It is a process of understanding, examining, and explicating the meaning, nature, and functioning of being human for African people by conducting a deep, profound, and penetrating search, study, and mastery of the process of "illuminating" the human spirit and the totality of all human experiences and phenomena. Skh Djr operates from the basic premise that there is an African way of being that reflects an African quality of thought

---

[1]See, Nobles, W.W. 2015. From Black psychology to *Sakhu Djaer*: Implications for the further development of a Pan African Black psychology. *Journal of Black Psychology* 41: 399–414. DOI: https://doi.org/10.1177/0095798413478072

and practice. The criterion of Pan-African (Black) psychology's, ergo, Skh Djr's evolution speaks to authenticity, the liberation of the African mind, empowerment of the African character, and enlivenment and illumination of the African spirit.

As noted, the term *Skh Djr* derives from the ancient Kemetian language, where *Skh* (sḥw) signifies the illumined or awakened spirit, and *Djr* (dr) denotes flow, movement, and continuity. Together, Skh Djr embodies the idea of "being in flow as an illumined spirit." It advances the understanding that human beings are not static entities but are divine energy in constant becoming. This metaphysical notion rejects Cartesian dualism and material reductionism, asserting instead that true being is spirit and eternally evolving. As noted, "Skh is not a thing. It is the process of becoming. Djr speaks to the flow of that becoming, as in the rivers of life that are constantly moving, reshaping, and carrying us" (p. 36).

Skh Djr challenges the Western assumption of objectivity and separateness by framing knowledge as the result of spirit alignment and communal resonance. The research process, in this model, becomes a sacred act of realignment with ancestral memory, cosmic rhythm, and collective destiny. Knowledge, therefore, is not merely accumulated but spirit remembered. The research process in this model becomes a sacred act of realignment with ancestral memory, cosmic rhythm, and collective destiny. Knowledge, therefore, is not merely accumulated but spiritually remembered.

Evolutionary genesis is the modern articulation of sꜣḫw r sꜣḫw. It is the praxis of spiraling toward light using the ancestral light we already carry. In research, clinical, educational, and political contexts, this synthesis carries transformative implications. For example, in education, it means pedagogy must begin from the ancestral light of the student, not from Eurocentric assumptions.

Teaching becomes an act of "illuminating the illumined," not depositing foreign knowledge. In healing practices, it affirms that the client is already sacred (DEMM), and restoration involves reanimating dormant ancestral frequencies rather than imposing diagnostic categories. In leadership and governance, it insists on ancestral authority, cultural continuity, and Zola–Ngolo (vital impulse) to guide visionary institutions that serve future generations.

Skh Djr, as sꜣḥw r sꜣḥw, and "evolutionary genesis" represent a revolutionary reimagining of research and knowledge production from an African-centered perspective. By grounding knowing in spiritness, ancestral memory, and cosmic rhythm, they restore dignity, depth, and divinity to the act of inquiry. These frameworks move beyond critique and offer a constructive, coherent, and culturally sovereign approach to knowledge. In doing so, researchers should activate the illumined soul for the healing and advancement of African people. As a bridge to the exploratory African-centered congruent research methodology, sꜣḥw r sꜣḥw and "evolutionary genesis" position Africana research as a sacred covenant to remember, restore, and re-soul the path of knowing.

Evolutionary genesis is the methodological counterpart to the ontological framework of Skh Djr. It is a threefold process: reclamation, refinement, and restoration. Reclamation involves recovering ancestral knowledge from oral traditions, cosmologies, rituals, and embodied practices. Refinement refers to integrating these ancestral insights with contemporary scientific and metaphysical tools, such as quantum theory, epigenetics, or vibrational medicine. Restoration emphasizes reintegrating these knowings into African life worlds to foster personal, communal, and cosmic wellness. Through evolutionary genesis, research is transformed into a living dialogue between the past, the present, and the future. It replaces the Western scientific model of extraction and control with a rhythmic process of spirit-led inquiry and reconnection. "Knowing is not just cognitive. It is rhythmic, embodied, and spirit-defined. Evolutionary genesis insists that knowledge is remembered, not discovered" (p. 89).

Both $s^i\underline{h}w$ r $s^i\underline{h}w$ and evolutionary genesis signify a fundamental shift in the ontological, epistemological, and methodological foundations of the research enterprise: These frameworks disrupt the colonized epistemic order and replace it with a re-ontology and re-epistemology of an African way of knowing that honors the sacred, the ancestral, and the cosmic. The integrative nature of $s^i\underline{h}w$ r $s^i\underline{h}w$ and evolutionary genesis lays the foundation for a mode of inquiry that is ontologically grounded in African spirit being, epistemologically anchored in ancestral memory, and methodologically guided by coherence, rhythm, and relational integrity. It is African-centered because it emerges from within African cosmological and cultural frameworks, not imposed from without. It is congruent because it seeks alignment between the knower, the known, and the process of knowing—a tripartite relationship mediated through spirit, symbol, and sacred space.

The key features of $s^i\underline{h}w$ r $s^i\underline{h}w$ and evolutionary genesis should include Bio-Phonic communications that recognizes that knowledge may emerge through vibrational resonance across realms (e.g., dreams, spirit messages, ritual enactments); Noetic Sensoria that utilizes African sensory systems that privilege intuitive, rhythmic, and energetic knowing; Ancestral dialogics that structures research as a conversation with the ancestors, incorporating divination, story-circles, and oral testimonies guiding the research process through cycles of movement, tension, and release, mirroring cosmic and communal rhythms;

and Sakhu activation that frames research not as data collection but as a process of illuminating the soul for the healing of the people.

The ultimate aim of *sᵌḫw r sᵌḫw* and evolutionary genesis is not to produce generalizable knowledge in the Western sense but to restore alignment between the visible and invisible realms, and to mend disconnections within the interlocking rings of being. It is, in my opinion, to fearlessly engage in exploratory considerations that assist in the reintroduction of ancestral memes that restore coherence in African consciousness and Black identity, strengthen familial purpose and destiny, engage in energetic rhythmic ancestral sound and motion, and interrogate astral dream visitations and energetic resonance along with exploring the idea of epigenetics of the invisible.

sᵌḫw r sᵌḫw and evolutionary genesis are offered as the foundational catalytic episteme[2] that guides a radical return to ancestral coherence. It serves not merely as a philosophical idea, but as a paradigm shifting episteme, a living process of reclaiming, refining, and regenerating African wisdom across both the visible and invisible realms of reality. As proposed, this catalytic episteme represents a revolution in knowing. Rather than a linear, extractive model of acquiring information, it is a spiral process of becoming, rooted in ancestral memory and cosmological

---

[2] "Foundational catalytic episteme" represents a spirit-defined framework of knowing that forms the essential basis for African-centered consciousness, and which activates profound paradigm shifts, generates new language, revitalizes ancestral practices, and reestablishes divine alignment between the seen and unseen realms of reality. It should be thought of as generative, dynamic, and transformative causing or accelerating transformation; initiating or energizing systemic change. "Catalytic" asserts that evolutionary genesis is not static. It is an agent of change that triggers movement, reorganization, and elevation in the epistemological field.

alignment. It is through *sⁱḥw r sⁱḥw* and evolutionary genesis that epistemic dislocations caused by colonization, enslavement, and cultural misorientation can be mended. *sⁱḥw r sⁱḥw* and evolutionary genesis involves moving from mechanistic science to holistic science of being; prioritizing ancestral memory, spirit-defined resonance, and moral alignment over detached empiricism; and interpreting reality as multi-realms of reality, encompassing both material and immaterial dimensions. *sⁱḥw r sⁱḥw* and evolutionary genesis decolonize not only content but the very structure of how knowledge is produced, validated, and transmitted. They reinsert spirit as central to inquiry, and in doing so, realign the pursuit of knowledge with the divine order (Ma'at, Kimuntu, Ubuntu).

sⁱḥw r sⁱḥw and evolutionary genesis are, therefore, best understood as the *epistemic* catalytic *process of rescuing, reclaiming, and refining* ancient African thought, wisdom traditions, and cosmological principles to guide the ongoing, organic unfolding of new concepts, methods, and frameworks. It centers African ways of knowing, being, and doing as genesis (not relics) for contemporary investigation and innovation. It should function both as a methodology for research and respirited definition and a cosmological orientation that understands being, knowing, and reality as spirit continuously becoming.

Once the process of rescue is underway, *reclaiming* involves asserting ownership over these bodies of knowledge and positioning them within a contemporary framework. In doing so, *sⁱḥw r sⁱḥw* and evolutionary genesis fosters epistemic integrity, a fidelity to African thought as an authentic source of knowing. This reclamation serves as a counter to what Kobi Kambon (1998) identified as cultural misorientation, a psychological condition in which African-ascended peoples adopt alien (Western) paradigms to their own detriment. Reclaiming ensures that these intellectual traditions are not viewed merely as historical artifacts but as relevant and applicable frameworks for current challenges in human development. Epistemic integrity in the *sᵌḥw r sᵌḥw* and evolutionary genesis model also implies an interrogation of Western knowledge production, which, as pointed out by Sylvia Wynter et al. (1995), often excludes or distorts non-Western cosmologies. In essence, reclaiming knowledge is an act of ensuring fidelity to the original African epistemic reflections while allowing them to inform contemporary discourse, thereby maintaining their authenticity, refinement, and cultural congruency.

Refining refers to the iterative process of critically evaluating, modifying, and adapting ancient African thought for use in modern contexts. Through this process, the concept of *sᵌḥw r sᵌḥw* and evolutionary genesis distinguishes itself from static notions of tradition and/or Western framed grounded theory. Ancient African thought is not merely preserved but is actively engaged with, tested, and refined to meet the demands of contemporary intellectual, cultural, and material conditions. This process of refinement is in keeping with the works of African-centered thinkers like Na'im Akbar (2004), who argue that African knowledge systems must continue to evolve to retain their relevance in addressing modern existential challenges. Refinement also reflects what is often referred to as the "Sankofa principle," which advocates a forward-looking return to the past. The organic development of thought involves both a return to ancestral wisdom and a projection into the future, where African knowledge systems guide the unfolding of new ideas, methods, and programs.

By allowing ancient African thought to guide the generation of new ideas and practices, *sᵌḥw r sᵌḥw* and evolutionary genesis provide a robust epistemological and practical foundation for the ongoing unfolding of concepts, theories, and services that resonate with African-ascended populations globally.

Rather than applying Eurocentric ontologies to African phenomena, evolutionary genesis returns to African cosmology (e.g., Bantu–Kongo, Yoruba, Akan) as first wisdom. It shifts the locus of analysis from the *dissected individual* to the *interconnected collective self* across realms. Where Western science often values fixed laws, *sꜣḫw r sꜣḫw* and evolutionary genesis emphasize processual growth (*asili, ntanda*) and the unfolding and manifestation of spirit in new forms, reflecting the "continuum of being." *sꜣḫw r sꜣḫw* and evolutionary genesis will allow for multidimensional research that is capable of tracing how trauma or wisdom travels across generations through genetic memory, ancestral whispers, ritual, or spirit possession.

I believe that to investigate this integrative vision of being spirit, Africana research must draw upon traditional African epistemologies, quantum metaphysics, and transdisciplinary methods. This research paradigm for understanding being spirit offers a way to study the spirit core of existence as emergent, interconnected, and continuous across realms.

Africana research should, ipso facto, be vested in the inquiry of spirit being, not merely in the material or psychological dimensions of human life, but in the *Spirit(ness)* of human experience as DEMM. *sꜣḫw r sꜣḫw* and evolutionary genesis are core. This research paradigm is guided by a research philosophy that transcends Eurocentric binaries of mind–body, subject–object, and science–religion by anchoring inquiry in the multidimensional continuum of reality (visible and invisible). The paradigm reclaims ancestral ways of knowing, reorients inquiry through ontological consciousness, and centers the unfolding of being as a spirit-driven and spirit-defined cosmic process.

Accordingly, *sꜣḫw r sꜣḫw* and evolutionary genesis would expand the scope of research to include elements such as ancestral energy, spirit resonance, and the divine flow of energy as variables that shape human behavior, consciousness, and societal functioning. Theoretical frameworks based on spirit(ness) and DEMM might draw on indigenous African epistemologies, which emphasize interconnection, healing, and the cyclical nature of life. For instance, a theory could be constructed that views human behavior not as isolated actions but as an ongoing interaction between the physical self, ancestral spirits, and divine energies. Hence, in integrating spirit(ness) and DEMM into new theory construction, sample selection, hypothesis generation, data analysis, and interpretation offer a holistic paradigm for understanding the interconnectedness of all beings and the role of spirit in human existence. This approach allows for the inclusion of both visible and invisible factors in the study of human behavior and well-being, providing a more complete picture of reality. By incorporating African-centered epistemologies, quantum principles such as entanglement, and indigenous spirit-defined practices, this framework challenges the boundaries of traditional science and opens new avenues for healing, personal transformation, and community empowerment.

Theories rooted in spirit(ness) and DEMM challenge the foundational assumptions of conventional scientific thought. To build new theories that incorporate these concepts, one must begin with the premise that reality is not divided into neatly segregated physical and spirit-defined domains. Instead, human beings are viewed as dynamic spirit beings, interconnected with both the seen and unseen forces of the universe. This conceptualization aligns with the idea that spirit(ness) is not just a mental or psychological attribute but a fundamental component of the human experience that interacts with the material world in profound ways.

New Africana research grounded in spirit(ness) and DEMM might also draw from quantum mechanics' ideas of entanglement and resonance, suggesting that individuals are "entangled" within a spirit-defined web of familial, community, and ancestral influences. This theory would, therefore, challenge the traditional, linear models of causality and propose a more fluid, dynamic interaction between the visible and invisible realms.

Understanding being spirit through s^{j}ḫw r s^{j}ḫw and evolutionary genesis is an act of epistemic justice and cultural restoration. It is not merely a theoretical stance, but a call to *remember* who we are as DEMM. In this framework, spirit is not studied from afar. It is alive and *lived, echoed, and co-created* across time, space, and ancestral continuum.

s^{j}ḫw r s^{j}ḫw and evolutionary genesis offers Africana researchers as spirit-defined mandate: to listen with the soul, to see with ancestral eyes, and to speak with tongues of flame. This is the praxis of becoming. This is the spirit-defined science of being spirit. The integration of spirit(ness) and DEMM into new theory construction, sample selection, hypothesis generation, data analysis, and interpretation requires paradigm shifting that incorporates both immaterial (invisible) and material (visible) perspectives. African-centered theories, such as those concerning spirit(ness) and DEMM, will offer a unique lens through which one can develop research frameworks that challenge traditional Western methodologies, embracing a more holistic and interconnected understanding of reality.

The frameworks of s^{j}ḫw r s^{j}ḫw and evolutionary genesis represent a transformative reorientation of the research enterprise. These interrelated concepts provide not only a critique of Western epistemologies but also a restorative blueprint for reclaiming knowledge production rooted in African being, spirit, and cosmological continuity. Through s^{j}ḫw r s^{j}ḫw and evolutionary genesis, research is transformed into a living dialogue between the past, the present, and the future. It replaces the Western scientific model of extraction and control with a rhythmic process of spirit-led inquiry and reconnection. Knowing is not just cognitive. It is rhythmic, embodied, and spirit-defined.

Evolutionary genesis insists that knowledge is remembered, not discovered" (p. 89). These frameworks disrupt the colonized epistemic order and replace it with African way of knowing that honors the sacred, the ancestral, and the cosmic. The integrative nature of *sꜣ ḫw r sꜣ ḫw* and evolutionary genesis lays the foundation for a mode of inquiry that is ontologically grounded in African spirit being, epistemologically anchored in ancestral memory, and methodologically guided by coherence, rhythm, and relational integrity. As proposed, it is exploratory in that it resists finality and embraces the process of *becoming*. It is African-centered because it emerges from within African cosmological and cultural frameworks, not imposed from without. It is congruent because it seeks alignment between the knower, the known, and the process of knowing, a tripartite relationship mediated through spirit, symbol, and sacred space. Evolutionary genesis and Skh open the door for African researchers to reenter their own epistemic house and conduct research as a spiritual, ancestral, and communal act.

Thus, *sꜣ ḫw r sꜣ ḫw* and evolutionary genesis represent a revolutionary reimagining of research and knowledge production from an African-centered perspective. By grounding knowing in spiritness, ancestral memory, and cosmic rhythm, they restore dignity, depth, and divinity to the act of inquiry. These frameworks move beyond critique and offer a constructive, coherent, and culturally sovereign approach to knowledge. In doing so, they activate the *sakhu*—the illumined soul—for the healing and advancement of African people. As a bridge to the exploratory African-Centered congruent research methodology, they position African research as a sacred covenant to remember, restore, and re-soul the path of knowing.

In practice, *sꜣ ḫw r sꜣ ḫw* and evolutionary genesis form the philosophical and methodological foundation for African-centered research, restorative wellness, education, governance, and theory building. This includes (1) **Re-indigenizing Knowledge Systems:** designing curricula and research rooted in African cosmology, language, and memory (Obenga, 2004); (2) **Restorative Mental Health:** utilizing ancestral healing, Zaya discourse (memory + imagination), and DEMM-based diagnostics for wellness (Nobles, 2023); (3) **Cultural Sovereignty:** asserting African agency through reclaiming the sacredness of knowing and becoming, rather than adopting Eurocentric dichotomies; and (4) **Living Ma'at:** Both concepts demand ethical living (*serudja ta*)—reciprocal re-birthing—as part of becoming luminous and contributing to collective wellness. Finally, the utility of the concept of *sꜣḫw r sꜣḫw* and evolutionary genesis lies in its capacity to generate frameworks that are not only culturally congruent but also intellectually robust.

While this chapter frames *sꜣḫw r sꜣḫw* and evolutionary genesis as an exploratory research methodology through African eyes that guides researching the visible and invisible in SKH, the science of being, *sꜣḫw r sꜣḫw* and evolutionary genesis are more than methodology. It is African cosmological praxis. *sꜣḫw r sꜣḫw* and evolutionary genesis enable us to investigate the visible and invisible layers of African real(ity) as a unified continuum. They will allow us to listen for ancestral codes, observe their current expressions, and co-create (not merely document) the next iteration of being.

While this expository discussion is written with African-centered research methodologists in mind, *sꜣḫw r sꜣḫw* and evolutionary genesis have, I believe, importance for Global Pan-African development and sovereignty. *sꜣḫw r sꜣḫw* and evolutionary genesis allows African-centered practitioners and activists to treat governance as spirit-defined custodianship, rooted in spirit(ness) and DEMM; to aligns social institutions (education, health, governance) with ancestrally validated principles of justice, reciprocity, and energetic harmony; to prioritize community-centered models such as Ubuntu (Zulu), Kanda (Kongo), and Ojúmó ni ire (Yoruba) to drive development in education, family life, health care, governance, and personal and collective sovereignty.

The intent of this chapter was to explore the definitions, functions, and paradigm-shifting implications of *s꜌ḥw r s꜌ḥw* and evolutionary genesis as groundbreaking contributions to the Science of Being particularly within the Africana world. It should, however, be noted, as synopsis, that this discourse might be seen or judged, not as scientific, but as conjecture or highly speculative. It will be seen as conjectural or speculative only because our formal education has been limited to and/or shaped and defined by Westernization and an unchallenged loyalty to a western grand narrative that omitted the interrogation of non-Western thought, particularly African thought, and intellectual propositions. There is very little, if any, literature on the exposition of African scientific theoretical development or methodological treatise. Hence, it is apropos that this brief discourse is finding its way in a little Black Book.

HOW TO DO *S꜌Ḥ W R S꜌Ḥ W* AND *EVOLUTIONARY GENESIS*

Step 1: Reconnection to African Genesis (Epistemic Rooting)

- Begin with cosmological narratives (Dogon Sirius wisdom, Kongo cosmogram, Yoruba *ase*).
- Activate Zaya Discourse (memory + imagination) to access ancestral codes and precolonial categories.

Step 2: Co-analysis Across Realms

- Examine signs in the visible realm (illness, misalignment, disunity).

- Investigate corresponding causes or disconnections in the invisible realm (ancestral neglect, spirit-defined contract violation, cosmological displacement).

Step 3: Spiral Reflection and Reinscription

- Use proverbs, dance, dreams, drumming, and spirit dialogue to spiral back into the source and bring forward new understandings or "evolved" forms.
- For example, a misalignment in *Kimuntu* (personhood) may emerge as illness, and through evolutionary genesis, this disease is realigned through ritual, ancestral re-affirmation, and community reintegration.

CHAPTER 3
We Are Spirit Beings

The phrase "We are spirit beings housed in a physical container having a human experience" encapsulates a profound spirit-defined truth deeply rooted in many African epistemologies and cosmologies. Across the vast expanse of African thought systems—such as the Yoruba, Bantu, Zulu, Wolof, Akan, Temne, Jolof, Ewe, and Dogon traditions—there is a common understanding that human beings are, first and foremost, spirit-defined entities. The physical body is seen as a temporary vessel or container for the spirit, which holds the true essence of existence.

Yoruba cosmology: In Yoruba cosmology, the term for spirit is Ori, which is the divine component of a person's existence. The Ori is more than just a person's "head" in the physical sense; it represents the individual's spirit-defined identity and destiny, chosen before birth. The Ara (body) is considered the temporary container for the Ori, and through it, the spirit-defined essence manifests in the physical realm. The Yoruba worldview asserts that the Ori is responsible for guiding an individual through life, helping to fulfill their divine purpose during their temporary human experience. Wande Abimbola emphasizes that "the Ori is more important than the body because it is the link to one's spirit-defined source and the divine" (Abimbola, 1976). In this context, we can say that we are Ori beings housed in physical bodies, navigating the human world.

BaKongo cosmology: In Bantu cosmology, particularly among the Bakongo and Luba peoples, the term Ntu is used to represent the vital life force or spirit that animates all beings. According to this worldview, Ntu is not confined to humans but exists in all living and nonliving entities, connecting them to the divine source. Placide Tempels describes Ntu as the "dynamic force of existence," which continues to thrive even after the physical body dies. For the Bantu, life is about maintaining harmony with the spirit-defined essence of Ntu while navigating the physical world (Tempels et al., 1959). Hence, human beings are Ntu beings housed in a physical form, temporarily experiencing life through the body.

Zulu Cosmology: In Zulu cosmology, the concept of Isithunzi and Umoya captures the idea of spirit. Isithunzi refers to the "shadow" or spirit-defined presence of a person, while Umoya means "breath" or "spirit" that gives life. The Zulu people believe that Umoya comes from Nkulunkulu, the Great Spirit, who breathes life into all beings. The physical body is seen as a temporary vessel that carries the Umoya, which is eternal and divine. After death, the Umoya continues to exist in the ancestral realm, interacting with the living. This understanding reinforces the notion that we are Umoya beings, housed in physical bodies, participating in the human experience as part of a larger spirit-defined journey (Ramose, 1999).

Wolof and Serer Cosmology: Among the Wolof and Serer peoples of Senegal, the term Ndox is often used to describe the spirit, while the Serer people use Jom to refer to a person's spirit-defined essence. Ndox, which literally means "water," symbolizes the fluid and eternal nature of the spirit. The Wolof believe that Ndox exists before birth and continues after physical death, much like a river flowing from one form to another. Jom, in Serer cosmology, represents the integrity and spirit-defined force of a person, which transcends the physical plane. The body is merely a temporary container for Ndox or Jom, and upon death, the spirit returns to the divine source (Diouf, 1998). In this sense, we are Ndox or Jom beings housed in physical containers, navigating the material world through our human experiences.

Akan Cosmology: In Akan thought, the Okra and Sunsum represent the spirit-defined components of a person. The Okra is considered the divine spark, or soul, directly emanating from Nyame (the Supreme Creator). It is eternal, preexisting birth and continues after death. The Sunsum refers to the spirit-defined personality, the part of a person that interacts with the physical world and can influence their character and actions. Both the Okra and Sunsum emphasize the Akan belief in a dual existence: The physical body is a temporary housing for the Okra, which is the true essence of a person. Upon death, the Okra returns to Nyame, affirming the spirit-defined continuity of life (Gyekye, 1995). We are, thus, Okra beings, housed in physical containers, experiencing the human journey through our Sunsum.

Temne and Jolof Cosmology: Among the Temne people, the Kanu is the spirit that animates the body. The Temne believe that Kanu is eternal and continues after the physical body dies. Similarly, the Jolof people use the term Nit ku bon, meaning "good soul," to describe the spirit-defined aspect of a person. Both cultures emphasize that the physical body is a temporary vessel for the Kanu or Nit ku bon and that the spirit exists before birth and after death, continuing its journey in the spirit-defined realm (Mbiti, 1969).

Ewe Cosmology: The Ewe people of Ghana and Togo use the term Se to describe the vital life force or spirit that animates all living beings. In Ewe cosmology, Se is a fragment of Mawu, the supreme deity, bestowed upon each individual to guide them through their earthly existence. The physical body is viewed as a temporary container for the Se, which transcends the material world. Upon death, the Se returns to Mawu, continuing its spirit-defined journey. This reflects the Ewe belief that we are fundamentally Se beings housed in physical containers, with the human experience serving as a chapter in a larger cosmic narrative (Greene, 2002).

Dogon Cosmology: In Dogon cosmology, the Nommo is the spirit-defined essence that connects all beings to the divine creator, Amma. The Nommo is often depicted as a primordial being or life force that brings order to the universe. The Dogon believe that each person is imbued with Nommo, which animates the body and guides them through life. After physical death, the Nommo continues its journey in the spirit-defined realm, affirming the Dogon belief in the cyclical nature of existence. The body is seen as a temporary housing for the Nommo, and life is viewed as a spiral journey of the spirit through various planes of existence (Griaule, 1965). Thus, we are Nommo beings, housed in physical containers, experiencing life through the lens of human consciousness.

African American cosmology: At the heart of African American spirit-defined cosmology lies a deeply rooted belief that human existence is fundamentally spiritual. This worldview, resonant with ancestral African cosmologies, understands the physical body not as the source of identity, but as a temporary vessel through which the eternal spirit expresses itself in the material realm. Across generations, African Americans have preserved and rearticulated this understanding through church traditions, ancestor reverence, music, dreams, healing rituals, and everyday speech. Phrases like "going home," "touched by the Spirit," and "feeling it in my soul" are not mere idioms but living affirmations of an enduring African epistemology that prioritizes spirit over flesh, eternity over temporality, and connection to the unseen over material detachment. This cosmology serves not only as a source of resilience and cultural continuity but also as a framework for navigating, understanding, and transforming lived experiences in a world that often denies the sacredness of Black life. In this way, the African American belief in being spirit beings housed in a physical body reflects a sacred inheritance, a spiritual intelligence that resists erasure and affirms the divine essence of being.

In other African diasporan Cosmologies (Vodou, Candomblé, and Santería), the African understanding of human beings as spiritual entities temporarily inhabiting physical form remains central. These traditions affirm that the essence of life is spirit (*lwa*, *orixás*, *santos*), and the human body is a vessel through which divine energy flows and manifests.

Haitian (Vodou) cosmology: In the experience of *possession* (being "mounted" by the lwa), where the spirit rides the body like a horse (*chwal*). The body becomes a sacred conduit for communication, healing, and transformation, reflecting the belief that the spirit world is not separate but intertwined with daily life. In Vodou, the body becomes a sacred site for divine possession. The *lwa* "mount" the initiate and speak through them, revealing that the spirit realm and material realm coexist in constant interaction.

Afro-Brazilian (Candomblé) cosmology: It expresses this through ritual embodiment of the orixás (spiritual forces of nature), where initiates (*filhos de santo*) undergo *incorporation*, allowing spirit to manifest through sacred dance, song, and drumming. The physical body is prepared, consecrated, and ritually aligned with the invisible realm to make spirit expression possible. In Candomblé, the embodiment of the *orixás* through trance and dance affirms that the spirit does not merely influence the body, but animates and speaks through it.

Afro-Cuban (Santería) cosmology (La Regla de Ocha): This belief is manifested in the *asiento* (spiritual enthronement), where the orisha is "seated" in the initiate's head. The head (*ori*) is considered the sacred dwelling of the divine, and the body becomes a spiritual house through which one's destiny (*iyanifa, babalao*) is fulfilled. In Santería, the ritual of *asiento* enthrones the orisha in the initiate's head, making the human person a living shrine of spirit.

Vodou, Candomblé, and Santería each affirms a sacred cosmology in which the human being is first and foremost a spirit—divine energy—temporarily clothed in flesh. These Afro-diasporic traditions, rooted in Yoruba, Fon, Kongo, and other African spiritual systems, uphold that life is not defined by the material body but by the eternal essence of spirit, which precedes birth and continues beyond death. The physical body is honored not as the center of identity, but as a vessel, a house, or a mount through which spiritual forces—*lwa, orixás, santos*—express themselves and fulfill divine purpose. These traditions preserve the African principle that spirit defines existence, not the physical form. They offer a living testimony that being is spiritual before it is biological and that the highest fulfillment of life is the alignment of the visible self with the invisible source.

Across the diverse cultures of the Yoruba, Bantu, Zulu, Wolof, Akan, Temne, Jolof, Ewe, and Dogon, African American, Haitian, Brazilian and Cuban peoples, the understanding of human existence is rooted in the notion that we are spirit-defined beings, temporarily housed in physical bodies. Within the collective African understanding of spirit and humanity, the body serves as a vehicle for the spirit, whether it is the Ori, Ntu, Umoya, Ndox, Okra, Kanu, Se, or Nommo, allowing us to navigate the material world and fulfill our spirit-defined purpose. These African philosophies highlight the idea that life is a continuum, with the human experience serving as just one phase in the journey of the spirit. The physical world is temporary, while the spirit is eternal, emphasizing that our true essence lies beyond the material realm. We are spirit beings having a human experience, temporarily housed in physical containers, as part of a much larger cosmic design.

In the global Pan-African world, the understanding of human existence is deeply spirit-defined. The body is viewed as a temporary vessel that houses the spirit during its journey on the physical plane. The ultimate essence of a person is not confined to the material world; rather, it is rooted in a divine, eternal source. These African epistemologies affirm the belief that we are spirit beings having a human experience, temporarily housed in a physical container as part of a much larger spirit journey.

CHAPTER 4

Being Spirit(ness)

The Heart of African-Centered Research

With understanding, spiritness, knowing, and knowledge production emerges from relationships, within oneself, within one's family, and within one's community. By interweaving practices that address all three "rings," an experiential space (the inner core) is created that nourishes confidence, competence, and a sense of limitless capacity. Upon facilitating these shared, meaningful experiences, we invite participants to recognize and sustain the interconnectedness of the visible and invisible realms that underpin true holistic reality. By focusing intentionally on the overlapping core of personhood, familyhood, and neighborhood, we unlock the synergy and "tone" of wellness that resonates throughout all levels of life. In this shared center, individuals experience a heightened clarity of purpose, deeper relationships, and a supportive, uplifting community. It is here that the visible and invisible realms meet, empowering us to live with confidence and cultivate limitless potential in ourselves and those around us. When these circles remain robust and actively intersect, the core becomes a generative space of wellness, constant in its capacity to renew, inspire, and guide persons, families, and entire communities to a fuller sense of confidence, competence, and possibility.

The experience of wellness reaffirms that each of us is part of something larger than ourselves. In that realization, confidence, competence, and a sense of full possibility emerge as the living, breathing reality of a whole/well community.

Synergy of the Three Rings: When each "ring" (personhood, familyhood, and neighborhood) is activated, they form a synergy in the overlapping core—an alchemical "sweet spot" or "tone" that gives rise to a "shared purpose" where personhood feels personally fulfilled, families thrive through strong bonds and shared values, and neighborhoods offer a sense of collective belonging. In this overlapping core, a person's sense of identity, relationship, and community reverberate through one another, creating synergy that is greater than the sum of its parts. "Resilience and support" where challenges become shared endeavors. Personal stress is supported by family rituals and neighborly goodwill, ensuring that neither the individual nor the group is left isolated. This mutual reinforcement help to face life's ups and downs with greater confidence and competence and an "expanded sense of possibility" that taps into the overlapping core highlights the seamless blending of visible and invisible realms—where intangible feelings of hope, love, or inspiration materialize through tangible community or family activities. This convergence nourishes the sense that one's potential is limitless, buoyed by collective support.

Tone as a Bridge: The "tone" of wellness, in this regard, is an experiential feeling that is both intuitive and visceral and lives at this core overlap. Tone serves as a bridge connecting personhood, familyhood dynamics, and neighborhood as recognizable emotion and energy. When the tone is nurtured in one ring, it naturally resonates in the others. As personhood tone, it is a feeling of inner calm, creativity, or empowerment that ripples outward into the family and community. As family tone, it can be seen as healthy communication, shared traditions, and mutual respect that amplifies personal well-being capable of extending hospitality and warmth to the broader neighborhood. Neighborhood tone is evidenced by inclusive celebrations, deep respect and high regard for excellence, communal care, and purposeful gatherings that bolster family ties and personal growth. By intentionally activating and/or cultivating this tone in community gatherings, family rituals, or personal practices, the sense of well-being is heightened, and the whole ecosystem thrives.

This activation should be a "multigenerational collaboration." For example, a neighborhood garden project is an ideal multigenerational collaboration of elders sharing knowledge of cultivation, parents organizing logistics, and children participating in planting especially when each participant contributes a unique strength, fostering interdependence and creating a palpable sense of shared success and joy. Multigenerational collaborations cause an overlapping and greater intensification of wellness at the core.

Family and community storytelling circles are powerful "activators." Storytelling, where individuals share their personal stories, cultural traditions, or life lessons, resonates on a personal level (self-reflection), a familial level (shared heritage), and a communal level (bonding through collective narratives). The confluence of these levels deepens trust and empathy across the entire group. Gather persons and families to engage in collective visioning, and Zaya Discourse dedicated to community growth and wellness is to have intentional "dreams" about the future of their neighborhood—identifying community projects, setting goals, and establishing support networks. In so doing, each voice is honored, personal passions aligned with family needs and community aspirations. The shared vision crystallizes in the core overlap, setting the stage for ongoing collective engagement.

Vibrant Vital Overlapping Core: To keep the overlapping core vibrant, it is important that any new initiative or practice be nurtured to reflect each circle's values and strengths. Encourage reflective and creative practices that help individuals (personal alignment) stay connected to their intuition, resilience, and personal vision of wholeness. Maintain ongoing communication through meaningful rituals (family check-ins, shared meals, and celebrations) that sustain families' integration and ensure harmony and togetherness. Intentionally design and support events and groups that foster inclusivity and mutual respect (community engagement), ensuring that neighborhood relationships remain strong, welcoming, and cohesive.

CHAPTER 5
The Real(ity)—The Visible and Invisible

This chapter is offered to illuminate a fuller appreciation of the realms of reality and thereby open up a wider more expansive canvas for engaging in African-centered research, especially as grounded in *sᵢḥw r sᵢḥw* and evolutionary genesis. In *SKH, From Black Psychology to the Science of Being*, the cosmos is understood as composed of interconnected, interdependent, and interpenetrating realms of reality—visible (material) and invisible (immaterial). This is consistent with classical African cosmology, which sees reality as a unified field (Fu-Kiau, 1991; Nobles, 2023). African epistemologies do not bifurcate the real into separate ontologies of physical versus spiritual. Rather, real(ity) is understood as layered, fluid, and interconnected. The "full African real(ity)" includes the visible realm (material/manifest), that which is the observable world: land, bodies, language, rituals, behavior. It includes memory embodied in oral traditions, architecture, dance, dress, food habits. African real(ity) also includes invisible realm (immaterial/spirit/ancestral). It encompasses ancestral consciousness, divine intelligence, sacred memory, bioenergetics and even the unseen forces such as destiny (*orí*), spiritual contracts,

DEMM, and communal coherence. *sᵗḥw r sᵗḥw* and evolutionary genesis enables a trans-realm analysis, allowing researchers and healers to simultaneously examine physical symptoms and metaphysical causes, cultural ruptures, and spiritual echoes.

The visible realm refers to the physical, material, and externally observable aspects of life—rituals, traditions, gatherings, and tangible actions. In a community context, this realm encompasses the sights, sounds, and structures we create: potluck dinners, family reunions, neighborhood events, group art projects, and the everyday gestures of helping one another. The invisible realm comprises the intangible, subtle energies, emotions, and intuitive insights that are not directly measurable by our senses. These include love, hope, compassion, aspirations, spiritual resonance, and the felt sense of connection. Also included are the collective moods, cultural beliefs, and shared values that shape a community's "tone," yet often remain hidden beneath the surface. When these two realms are in harmony, they co-create a palpable sense of spirit—a motivating, sustaining force that animates our shared existence.

The spiritness is revealed in the divine dance between the seamless visible and invisible realms of reality (see the Appendix for examples) as represented or reflected as personhood, familyhood, and neighborhood. It is at the central core of the three rings of wellness where personhood, familyhood, and neighborhood overlap that wellness is located. The invisible dimension of the personhood ring illustrates wellness as personal beliefs, innate gifts, dreams, and inner stirrings of purpose and drive for perfection. These guide one's sense of identity and self-worth. At the visible dimension, the personhood ring reflects physical self-care practices, creative pursuits, good speech, and outward behaviors that align with one's internal compass. Personhood meeting at the inner core supports personal authenticity (invisible) expressed in tangible ways (visible) creating coherence between who we feel we are inside and how we show up in the world.

The invisible dimension of familyhood illustrates Zaya (love), loyalty, trust, empathy, and unspoken traditions passed down through generations. Familyhood at the visible dimension is revealed by shared meals, family storytelling, communal problem-solving, celebratory gatherings, and the comforting routines that bring everyone together. Familyhood at the core supports the intangible ties (invisible) that find shape in family rituals (visible). The family becomes a vessel where inner values are perpetuated through supportive day-to-day interactions. The invisible dimension of neighborhood is indicated by the "tone" or feel of the community that represents collective spirit, shared vision, cultural attitudes, sense of belonging, and goodwill among neighbors. Neighborhood at the core supports the intangible ties (invisible) demonstrated in community gardens, art murals, volunteer initiatives, public celebrations, and collaborative learning spaces. Here, an undercurrent of neighborly care and local pride (invisible) is made real in public projects and gatherings (visible). A resilient vital neighborhood emerges from the shared energy of everyone who invests in it.

Within this overlapping core, where individual, familial, and communal energies intermingle, there is an ever-present spirit (energy) current. "Spirit," in this sense, does not necessarily denote a specific religious practice. Spirit as the "animating force" (1) invokes connections, (2) fosters compassion, (3) sparks inspiration, and (4) sustains resilience. By invoking connections, spirit animates the intrinsic connection as a unifying power that transcends personal differences, drawing us together in recognition of our mutual humanity. Fostering compassion is evidenced by the invisible empathy that takes visible expression as the spontaneous need to care for other. Our creative impulse to leap from the invisible to the visible innovative ideas for community engagement, personal growth, or family bonding is the third animating force of spirit that automatically supports the spirit of perseverance. At all times, the invisible support of oneness, compassion, inspiration, and resilience crystallizes into visible acts of solidarity and problem-solving.

When the visible and invisible realms flow together seamlessly, the spirit of a community becomes a constant source of life-affirming energy. In the inner overlapping core, (1) personhood feel empowered by a sense of self aligned with deeper truths; (2) familyhood flourish on a foundation of shared values and love; and (3) neighborhood blossom into vibrant, creative spaces where everyone is seen, heard, and valued.

The visible realm is the realm of matter, manifestation, and physical form. It includes everything that can be seen, heard, touched, measured, or empirically observed. However, in African-centered epistemology, the visible realm is not separate from the spirit, but is a *mirror or extension* of the invisible. The visible realm (material domain) includes measurable phenomena such as physical behaviors, environmental interactions, linguistic patterns, embodied cultural expressions, and neurobiological signatures of ancestral resonance (e.g., epigenetic markers, vocal inflection, rhythmic movement). See Key Component Grid below.

	Key Components
Component	Description
Body and Behavior	Includes physiological form, motor activity, somatic responses, posture, gestures. Example: illness in the body can reflect dis-harmony in the spirit
Language and Speech	Spoken word as a vibration of the soul; carries spiritual frequency
Physical Environment	Places, structures, tools, and objects shaped by culture and imbued with meaning
Ritual Performance	Embodied energetic practices like dance, drumming, libation as visible manifestations of spiritual continuity.
Cultural Expressions	Music, art, clothing, naming practices—all as expressions of invisible ancestral or cosmological values.
Neurobiological Traces	Expressions of ancestral memory in stress response, trauma signatures, or instinctual behavior

The invisible realm is the domain of spirit, energy, consciousness, memory, and intention. It encompasses metaphysical forces that shape behavior, identity, and being. This realm is considered primary in African cosmology—the source of life and meaning. The invisible informs the visible. The unseen governs the seen. The spirit dimension is the "mother of matter." The invisible realm (immaterial domain) includes spirit, metaphysical, and quantum-level phenomena like ancestral presence and transmission; intuitive and prophetic insight; bio-phonic and astral communication; energy fields (aura, coherence, resonance); and genetic memory and its influence on imagination and healing.

African-centered research methodologists should explore and consider the component descriptions identified with the identified citation listed below.

Key Components	
Component	Description
Spirit (Nzambi, Ori, Ntangu)	The life force and divine consciousness animating all things
Ancestral Presence	The continuing influence of the Yet-to-Live and the After-Living through guidance, dreams, and spiritual echoes
Bio-Phonic Communication	Spirit-sound frequency transmission between ancestors and the living
Memory and Imagination	Genetic memory and intuitive foresight as forms of ancestral energy and ancestral echo
Moral Coherence	Vibrational alignment between one's life and cosmic law (Ma'at), discernible in intuitive knowing and spiritual
Astral Resonance	Connections across time-space boundaries through ritual, meditation, or dreamwork

DEMM: STUDY POPULATION

The population in SKH-based evolutionary genetic research is not defined only by demographic categories (e.g., age, race, gender) alone but by states of being and levels of spiritual coherence. DEMM refers to humans as spirit beings encoded with divine intelligence, mission, and memory. Every research participant is therefore a *node of ancestral energy* existing in dynamic relation to all other beings, past and present. The population of interest in SKH research is not defined solely by identity markers, but by the spirit condition of being DEMM.

Population core: All African-ascended people, and by extension, all human beings, are considered DEMM (spirit beings) manifest in physical form, each carrying a mission, memory, and energy encoded in their being. "The African self is not separate from the divine. It is divine."

Spirit-defined awareness seeking and revealing experiences or transmission of ancestral memory; alignment or misalignment across personhood, familyhood, and neighborhood; and possessing evidence of spiritual disruption (e.g., Intergenerational Sensoria-Harm).

An expanded listing of population characteristics can be interrogated below.

Key Population Characteristics	
Characteristic	Description
Spirit-Nature (Essence)	Each participant is more than their flesh and is defined by their internal, divine spark
Cosmic Purpose	Life is lived not randomly but as part of a cosmological unfolding; each person has a role
Cultural Grounding	Participants may or may not be consciously grounded in African worldviews, but are spiritually connected through ancestral codes.
Trauma Imprints	Many DEMM beings carry intergenerational harm or psychic dislocation due to colonialism, slavery, or disconnection
Healing Capacity	Through rituals, memory work, and restoration, DEMM beings can realign with their essence
Vibrational Awareness	Capacity for spiritual attunement and engagement with invisible signals through dreams, vision, or intuitive alignment.

DEMM AS A POPULATION

- Children who exhibit ancestral knowledge or abilities without being taught
- Adults undergoing spirit reawakening through dream visitations
- Families who practice intergenerational naming and rituals
- Elders whose wisdom holds cosmological coherence
- Communities who sustain spiritual-cultural ecosystems of practice (e.g., drumming, libation, initiation rites).

Sampling should be purposeful and energetic, guided by vibrational coherence and ancestral resonance, rather than randomization.

Criteria for inclusion are as follows:

- Individuals with lived or inherited experiences of ancestral communication, bio-phonic healing, or spiritual memory recall
- Evidence of spiritual practices or traditions rooted in African cosmologies
- Representations across the interlocking rings of personhood, familyhood, and neighborhood.

Data collection instruments could include oral narratives and transgenerational memory interviews; bio-phonic or dream journal documentation; frequency/resonance mapping (via sound, vibration, heartbeat, tone); and ancestral pattern tracing through rites, names, and family rituals.

HYPOTHESIS GENERATION

In sᶦḥw r sᶦḥw and evolutionary genesis research, hypothesis generation is not abstract speculation but a revealed inquiry derived from ancestral whispering, intuition, and cosmological logic.

Sample hypotheses:

- "Those who engage in daily ancestral invocation exhibit greater coherence between visible and invisible behaviors."
- "Bio-phonic communication facilitates intergenerational healing and realignment of the energy field."
- "Naming practices rooted in ancestral lineages encode spiritual mission and influence moral behavior."

Hypotheses often reflect call-and-response formats:

- *Call*: Is the ancestral voice present in this generation?
- *Response*: How is the ancestral energy manifesting in the lives of the living?

Engaging Two Realms of Reality: In the visible realm, sample selection mirrors conventional methods—identifying individuals, families, communities, or neighborhoods based on observable traits, characteristics, or conditions. These may include the following:

- Sociocultural affiliations (e.g., African American, Afro-Brazilian, Wolof-speaking)
- Behavioral patterns
- Historical location or geospatial significance
- Demographics (age, gender, etc.)
- Responses to spirit-defined or ancestral dislocation

This is what might be called the **"witness of form,"** that is, those who bear evidence in the physical world of inherited or remembered cultural-spirit-defined continuity or disruption. In the invisible realm, sample selection is not random nor merely intuitive. It is spirit-guided, memory-evoked, and resonance-attuned. African thought acknowledges the "*Yet-to-Be*," the living, and the "*After-Living*," with the ancestral continuum communicating with, guiding, and influencing those in the material world. Thus, the dwellers in the invisible realm, ancestors, spirit-defined entities, unborn generations, and archetypal energies should be seen as informing who and what should be included in a sample for study.

HOW THE INVISIBLE REALM INFORMS SAMPLE SELECTION

- **Ancestral memory retrieval:** Individuals who experience dreams, visions, or inherited callings may be **identified by the ancestors** as those whose stories carry collective memory, trauma, or medicine. These individuals may not initially appear relevant from a traditional standpoint but are spirit-definedly "marked" as essential bearers of insight.

- **Bio-Phonic echoes:** Participants selected based on their resonance or sensitivity to **bio-phonic communications**—the spirit-defined "soundwaves" or impressions received through ritual, drumming, naming, or ancestral invocation—can be selected as carriers of **invisible frequencies of knowledge.**

- **Zaya discourse activation:** Sample selection may emerge through **Zaya Discourse** (dialogue between memory and imagination), where the researcher receives ancestral instruction, symbolic dreams, or intuitive recognitions of those who should be included in the inquiry.

- **Ritual and divination:** Traditional African sampling often includes consultation with oracles, diviners, or mediums, where spirit-defined technologies reveal who is cosmologically aligned to offer insight into a particular research question. In this way, selection is not only justified by empirical criteria but affirmed by spirit-defined authenticity.

Possible ways of selecting participants for a study on intergenerational memory loss:

- **Visible realm:** A researcher selects African-ascended participants who have experienced loss of cultural knowledge,
  language, or family histories.
- **Invisible realm:** Through libation, dream journaling, or divination, the researcher identifies three individuals whose
  ancestors have "shown themselves" repeatedly in rituals,
  requesting their family story to be told.
- **Result:** The final sample includes not only those with visible
  trauma but also those with ancestral permission and spirit-
  defined resonance (carriers of untold stories necessary to
  evolutionary genesis).

In a study on ancestral memory and spirit-defined healing,
sample selection could involve selecting individuals who have
demonstrated a deep connection to their ancestral heritage, such as
through cultural practices, familial rituals, or spirit-defined practices. These individuals may be more attuned to the energies and
ancestral wisdom that are central to the research. Additionally,
sampling could extend to populations that are not only based
on demographic factors such as race, age, and gender but also
spirit-defined and psychological factors, including levels of attunement to ancestral memory or spirit-defined resonance. Moreover,
in studies related to community wellness or ancestral healing, a
community-based participatory research (CBPR) approach may be
applied, where entire communities, rather than individuals alone,
are included as study participants. This is because the collective
energy of the community, the interconnections between persons,
family, and neighborhood, and the ancestral influences that shape
these communities are integral to understanding the whole.

DATA ANALYSIS AND INTERPRETATION

Data analysis incorporates both qualitative and energetic
modalities.

Analytical tools:

- Narrative analysis: Focused on ancestral motifs, symbols, and themes.
- Symbolic resonance analysis: Mapping sound, name, or color frequencies to ancestral traditions.
- Pattern recognition: Tracking recurring cosmological structures (triads, spirals, circles) in participant stories.
- Astral data coding: Interpreting dreams, visions, or spirit visitations as coded information systems.

Validation:

- Community interpretation circles
- Alignment with historical, linguistic, and cosmological knowledge
- Repetition or confirmation across multiple realms (dreams, rituals, behavior, and spoken words).

SUGGESTED RESEARCH AREAS AND INVESTIGATORY QUESTIONS

In any preliminary exploration of *s'ḥw r s'ḥw* and evolutionary genesis methodology, it is recommended that researchers locate their research initiatives as an act of restoration rather than extraction. It should seek understanding as the rebalancing of frequencies across time and space. Ultimately, it is a praxis enterprise that involves cocreating the activation of DEMM.

Personhood

Research areas are as follows:

- Identity formation through ancestral naming and spiritual invocation

- Dream recall and ancestral memory as sources of purpose
- Intergenerational trauma and vibrational dissonance
- Bio-phonic resonance and internal healing practices.

Investigatory questions are as follows:

- How do African-descended individuals retrieve and interpret ancestral memory through dreams or inner visions?
- What role does ancestral naming play in affirming identity and destiny?
- How does Zaya Discourse support spiritual reintegration in persons experiencing psychic fragmentation or dissociation?
- Can entangled memory patterns across siblings or cousins be traced through symbolic dreams and rituals?

Familyhood

The intention here should be to explain how these research areas are influenced by the invisible realm.

Research areas are as follows:

- Spiritual inheritance through family rituals, music, and symbols
- Collective dreaming and intergenerational communication
- Disruption and restoration of family rituals (e.g., libation, storytelling, drumming)
- Family-based healing circles and cosmological coherence.

Investigatory questions are as follows:

- How are spiritual memories passed down through maternal or paternal lines in diasporan families?
- In what ways do families experience "entangled healing" through shared spiritual practices?
- How does Zaya Discourse facilitate multigenerational meaning-making in families disrupted by migration, slavery, or displacement?

- What symbols, objects, or oral traditions act as carriers of ancestral energy in African-descended families?

Peoplehood

Research areas:

Investigatory questions are as follows:

- How do diasporan spiritual traditions reflect the ontological unity of African cosmologies?
- What are the cosmological patterns found in diasporan music, ritual, or dance that link back to specific African ethnic groups?
- Can Zaya Discourse be used to reconstruct cultural memory in communities affected by genocide, colonization, or displacement?
- In what ways does quantum entanglement mirror African understandings of spirit communication across time and space?

Wellness at the Intersecting Core

Ultimately, *sᵂḫw r sᵂḫw* and evolutionary genesis as reflected in Skh should explore the uncharted waters of inter-realm investigations.

Research areas: Epistemological, Ecological, and Moral Harmony

- Wellness as coherence across visible and invisible realms
- Restoration of balance using ancestral ethics and vibrational realignment
- Epistemological restoration through ancestral knowledge systems
- Interventions rooted in ancestral ecology, harmony, and moral order (Ma'at)

Investigatory questions:

- What are the measurable effects of ancestral ritual on psychological and emotional wellness?

- How can Zaya Discourse inform clinical practices for African-descended populations?
- In what ways does alignment with ancestral energy improve self-regulation and spiritual integrity?
- How does the restoration of personhood–familyhood–peoplehood through spiritual praxis affect community well-being?

SAMPLE RESEARCH AGENDA

The aim of this sample research agenda is to offer a preliminary sample for guiding the restorative coherence within the interconnecting rings of personhood, familyhood, and peoplehood with wellness located at their intersecting core.

Primary Goals

1. Restore ancestral memory and spiritual coherence in African-descended individuals and communities.
2. Establish a culturally grounded methodology (Zaya Discourse) for research across metaphysical and material domains.
3. Generate evidence-based practices for restoring personhood, familyhood, and peoplehood.
4. Engage Pan-African scholars and communities in quantum-informed, spiritually grounded research.

Domains

Personhood: Spirit being and inner coherence

- *Research Focus:* Identity formation, ancestral naming, internal coherence
- *Key Questions:*

o   How does ancestral naming impact purpose realization?
o   What role do dreams and inner visions play in affirming spiritual mission?
o   Can entangled memory events predict spiritual misalignment or healing?

Familyhood: Ancestral lineage and generational transmission

- *Research Focus:* Multigenerational healing, spiritual inheritance, collective dreaming
- *Key Questions:*
  o   How do families experience shared ancestral visions or symbols?
  o   In what ways does Zaya Discourse repair generational ruptures caused by migration or enslavement?
  o   What spiritual rituals act as containers of intergenerational wisdom?

Peoplehood: Collective memory and cultural purpose

- *Research focus:* Diasporan cultural echoes, cross-continental ritual alignment, spiritual identity
- *Key questions:*
  o   How do diasporan rituals reflect shared cosmologies across time and geography?
  o   What ancestral ethics are embedded in Africana art forms?
  o   Can Zaya Discourse reconstruct collective memory in post-genocidal or colonized communities?

Wellness at the intersecting core:

- *Research focus:* Ma'atic harmony, ecological and epistemological restoration

- *Key questions:*

  - What are the spiritual metrics of wellness in African-centered frameworks?
  - How does quantum resonance affirm moral and energetic alignment?
  - Can Zaya Discourse produce scalable healing interventions in community settings?

CHAPTER 6

A New Paradigm for Understanding Being Spirit

The integration of spirit(ness) and DEMM into new theory construction, sample selection, hypothesis generation, and data analysis. Interpretation require a paradigm shift that incorporates both spiritual and scientific perspectives. African-centered theories, such as those concerning spirit(ness) and DEMM, offer unique lenses through which we can develop research frameworks that challenge traditional Western methodologies, embracing a more holistic and interconnected understanding of reality. This section explores how these concepts can be operationalized within a scientific research context, addressing new theory construction, hypothesis generation, and data analysis methods. Again, the traditional research language and overall process should be filtered through the paradigm shifting ideas of *sᵌḥw r sᵌḥw* and evolutionary genesis, spirit being (DEMM) and realms of reality.

Theories rooted in spirit(ness) and DEMM challenge the foundational assumptions of conventional scientific thought. To build new theories that incorporate these concepts, one must begin with the premise that reality is not divided into neatly segregated physical and spiritual domains. Instead, human beings are viewed as dynamic spirit beings, interconnected with both the seen and unseen forces of the universe. This conceptualization aligns with the idea that spirit(ness) is not just a mental or psychological attribute but a fundamental component of the human experience that interacts with the material world in profound ways.

In theory construction, this approach expands the scope of research to include elements such as ancestral energy, spirit resonance, and the divine flow of energy as variables that shape human behavior, consciousness, and societal functioning. Theoretical frameworks based on spirit(ness) and DEMM might draw on indigenous African epistemologies, which emphasize interconnection, healing, and the cyclical nature of life. For instance, a theory could be constructed that views human behavior not as isolated actions but as an ongoing interaction between the physical self, ancestral spirits, and divine energies.

A new theory grounded in spirit(ness) and DEMM might also draw from quantum mechanics ideas of entanglement and resonance, suggesting that individuals are "entangled" within a spiritual web of familial, community, and ancestral influences. This theory would, therefore, challenge the traditional, linear models of causality and propose a more fluid, dynamic interaction between the visible and invisible realms.

The holistic approach: In traditional research methods, sample selection is often based on a random or convenience sampling model, focusing on the physical attributes of the population. However, when conducting research grounded in spirit(ness) and DEMM, sample selection would need to reflect the interconnected nature of human existence. This means that the selection of participants would be informed by both their visible (physical) attributes and their spirit-defined or ancestral connections. In the methodological framework of *Evolutionary genesis*, sample selection must encompass both the visible and invisible realms of reality. This dual-realm approach reflects the African cosmological understanding that reality is not solely defined by what is materially observable, but includes the spirit-defined, metaphysically attuned, and ancestrally guided dimensions that influence and shape human experience. Sample selection within evolutionary genesis honors the African imperative to consult both the material and the metaphysical, both empirical relevance and spirit-defined resonance. The visible realm offers the terrain; the invisible realm offers the divine map. True research rooted in African knowing is not only about observing the world but about being called into it by the world beyond. Thus, the dwellers in the invisible realm are not passive ghosts of the past, but active selectors of who must speak, remember, and carry the flame forward. In this way, evolutionary genesis transcends sampling as simple selection. It becomes sampling as spirit-defined restoration

Ancestral wisdom and energy dynamics: Hypothesis generation in the context of spirit(ness) and DEMM involves crafting research questions that consider the spirit-defined and energetic dimensions of human experience. Unlike traditional research, which often begins with hypotheses based on observable physical phenomena, hypotheses grounded in spirit(ness) and DEMM might focus on the unseen forces that influence human behavior and well-being.

For example, a hypothesis might be framed as: "*The alignment of individuals with ancestral memory and spirit-defined resonance will correlate with increased community wellness and personal healing outcomes.*" This hypothesis suggests that spirit-defined and ancestral connections are not peripheral to human experience but central to understanding psychological and social phenomena. Researchers may also hypothesize that astral resonance, the frequency at which individuals align with divine and ancestral energies, directly impacts their mental and physical health. Another hypothesis could focus on entanglement: "*Spirit-defined entanglement with ancestral and community energies enhances individual resilience in times of crisis, irrespective of material limitations.*" This hypothesis positions the invisible or spirit-defined realm as a fundamental source of strength that is linked to observable behaviors, suggesting that the entanglement of human spirits with the collective energy of community and ancestry can manifest in real-world benefits.

In traditional research methods, sample selection is often based on a random or convenience sampling model, focusing on the physical attributes of the population. However, when conducting research grounded in spirit(ness) and DEMM, sample selection would need to reflect the interconnected nature of human existence. This means that the selection of participants would be informed by both their visible (physical) attributes and their spiritual or ancestral connections.

For instance, in a study on ancestral memory and spiritual healing, sample selection could involve selecting individuals who have demonstrated a deep connection to their ancestral heritage, such as through cultural practices, familial rituals, or spiritual practices. These individuals may be more attuned to the energies and ancestral wisdom that are central to the research. Additionally, sampling could extend to populations that are not only based on demographic factors such as race, age, and gender but also spiritual and psychological factors, including levels of attunement to ancestral memory or spiritual resonance.

Moreover, in studies related to community wellness or ancestral healing, a CBPR approach may be applied, where entire communities, rather than individuals alone, are included as study participants. This is because the collective energy of the community, the interconnections between persons, family, and neighborhood, and the ancestral influences that shape these communities are integral to understanding the whole.

Hypothesis generation in the context of spirit(ness) and DEMM involves crafting research questions that consider the spiritual and energetic dimensions of human experience. Unlike traditional research, which often begins with hypotheses based on observable physical phenomena, hypotheses grounded in spirit(ness) and DEMM might focus on the unseen forces that influence human behavior and well-being. For example, a hypothesis might be framed as: *"The alignment of individuals with ancestral memory and spiritual resonance will correlate with increased community wellness and personal healing outcomes."* This hypothesis suggests that spiritual and ancestral connections are not peripheral to human experience but central to understanding psychological and social phenomena. Researchers may also hypothesize that astral resonance, the frequency at which individuals align with divine and ancestral energies, directly impacts their mental and physical health.

Another hypothesis could focus on entanglement. "Spiritual entanglement with ancestral and community energies enhances individual resilience in times of crisis, irrespective of material limitations." This hypothesis positions the invisible or spiritual realm as a fundamental source of strength that is linked to observable behaviors, suggesting that the entanglement of human spirits with the collective energy of community and ancestry can manifest in real-world benefits.

To analyze data within the context of spirit(ness) and DEMM, researchers may utilize mixed-methods approaches that combine quantitative and qualitative techniques. Qualitative data could include interviews, life histories, and spiritual experiences related to ancestral memory, while quantitative data might capture changes in health, wellness, and behavior through physiological measures, psychological assessments, and community engagement surveys. For instance, spiritual resonance could be assessed using qualitative techniques such as ethnographic observations, focus groups, and personal reflections to understand how individuals or communities experience their connection to ancestral memory. At the same time, quantitative tools could measure variables such as mental health outcomes, community cohesion, or resilience to trauma, providing a dual lens of analysis.

Researchers might also turn to bioenergetics and bio-photonics, which allow for the measurement of energy patterns within the human body. These tools could help quantify the "spiritual energy" or resonance that participants emit and how this aligns with their perceived connection to ancestral and divine energies. Data on astral resonance, energy fields, and changes in spiritual attunement might be gathered using tools such as electroencephalogram (EEG) readings or heart rate variability (HRV), linking spiritual dynamics to physical health outcomes.

Interpretation: Interpreting data derived from research on spirit(ness) and DEMM requires an approach that integrates both the visible and invisible realms. This means interpreting quantitative data in conjunction with qualitative insights into the participants' spiritual experiences, emotional responses, and cultural practices. The insights gained from studying ancestral memory, astral resonance, and entanglement may reveal complex interconnections between physical health, spiritual well-being, and social engagement that are not easily measurable through conventional scientific paradigms. For instance, the interpretation of data might reveal that individuals with stronger ancestral connections or higher levels of spiritual resonance exhibit greater psychological resilience or experience improved health outcomes following trauma or illness. The influence of **entanglement**—the interconnectedness of individuals with their communities and ancestors—might be seen in how spiritual practices, such as ritual and prayer, create observable shifts in collective well-being. In terms of knowing and knowledge acquisition write an expository essay explaining the difference and applications of gaining Insight Hindsight Foresight Oversight Nosight.

UNDERSTANDING THE DIMENSIONS OF KNOWING

Insight, hindsight, foresight, oversight, and no sight across visible and invisible realms of reality is essential to the process of knowing and knowledge production. Knowledge acquisition is not a monolithic process. It involves the dynamic interplay of time, perspective, consciousness, and engagement across visible and invisible realms of reality. Within African-centered epistemology, knowing is more than an intellectual act. It is a spiritual, ancestral, communal, and metaphysical engagement. This essay examines five distinct epistemic dimensions, hindsight, foresight, oversight, and no sight as modes of knowing and knowledge acquisition. Each functions differently across the visible (material) and invisible (immaterial) realms of reality and has implications for how we come to know, remember, anticipate, manage, and remain ignorant of phenomena in our lives.

Insight: Inner Seeing and Immediate Knowing

Definition: Insight is the deep and often sudden understanding of the nature of a thing. It is an intuitive grasp, often emerging from within, and involves penetrating beneath surface appearances.

Realm of Reality

- *Visible Realm:* Insight in the visible realm may appear as pattern recognition, emotional intelligence, or psychological clarity. It is when one reads a situation with precision without being told.
- *Invisible Realm:* In African traditions, insight is frequently spiritual—gained through dreams, rituals, ancestral messages, or divine intuition. This aligns with the concept of **s³ḥw** (sakhu)—the illumination of the heart-mind or "inner eye."

Application

Insight is crucial for *diagnosis* in healing traditions, decision-making in leadership, and moral discernment. For example, an elder may "see" the root of a child's behavioral issue not in behavior but in ancestral disturbance.

Hindsight: Reflective Knowing from the Past

Definition: Hindsight refers to understanding events after they have occurred. It is retrospective knowledge, often grounded in lessons learned.

Realm of Reality

- *Visible Realm:* Involves memory recall, experiential learning, or analysis of past records. This is foundational in historical studies and psychological self-assessment.
- *Invisible Realm:* Hindsight can emerge through ancestral memory or genetic memory. African spiritual systems teach that remembering is a sacred act—rekindling the *ka* (life force) of one's lineage and mistakes of the past.

Application

Hindsight supports the development of wisdom. It undergirds restorative practices, intergenerational healing, and corrections to epistemic and historical harms. It informs cultural revival, as seen in Africana remembering projects like *Sankofa*—"go back and fetch it."

Foresight: Anticipatory and Visionary Knowing

Definition: Foresight is the capacity to anticipate or envision future outcomes. It involves imaginative projection and spiritual preparedness.

Realm of Reality

- *Visible Realm:* Strategic planning, modeling, and extrapolation from current trends reflect foresight in visible domains.

- *Invisible Realm:* Prophecy, divination, and dream revelation constitute foresight in the immaterial domain. This is the work of the **Nganga** or seer in BaNtu traditions who perceives what is yet-to-manifest.

Application

Foresight governs *preventive care*, strategic governance, and vision-casting for personal and communal development. It allows for anticipatory healing, protection from harm, and moral direction rooted in ancestral teachings.

Oversight: Supervisory and Holistic Knowing

Definition: Oversight implies the capacity to see the whole, to monitor processes and ensure integrity or coherence in action.

Realm of Reality

- *Visible Realm:* Institutional leadership, quality control, and accountability structures use oversight to ensure alignment and performance.
- *Invisible Realm:* Oversight is also spiritual guardianship. Ancestors and spirits act as watchers, guiding and correcting the living. The notion of *Ma'at*—balance and order—is enforced through divine oversight.

Application

Oversight ensures relational, moral, and structural alignment. In African cosmology, a **community elder** or **council of sages** exercises oversight to maintain cosmic and social order. It is essential in familyhood, governance, and rites of passage.

No sight: Absence or Distortion of Knowing

Definition: Nosight refers to the state of unknowing, ignorance, or willful blindness. It is the failure or refusal to perceive what is evident or present.

Realm of Reality

- *Visible Realm:* Cognitive bias, denial, cultural amnesia, or miseducation can result in nosight.
- *Invisible Realm:* Nosight occurs when one's spirit is disconnected—when the inner light is dimmed or blocked, often due to trauma, colonial indoctrination, or disconnection from ancestral guidance.

Application

No sight manifests in *cultural misorientation*, fractured identity, and conceptual incarceration. Healing from no sight involves **restorative remembering**, cleansing rituals, and reconnection with spiritual and historical truths.

Interconnecting the Ways of Knowing

Each of the five ways of knowing—Insight, Hindsight, Foresight, Oversight, and No sight—functions within a **temporal-spiritual continuum** across the **visible and invisible realms.** They are not isolated processes but deeply intertwined in African-centered epistemology:

- *Insight* awakens in the present,
- *Hindsight* honors the past,
- *Foresight* prepares for the future,
- *Oversight* governs continuity,
- *No sight* signals disconnection and calls for healing.

Within the framework of evolutionary genesis and Skh (Science of Being), these dimensions become tools of reclaiming African ways of knowing, being, and becoming. By understanding and applying these epistemic modes, both individuals and communities can restore their wholeness, align with ancestral wisdom, and navigate the full spectrum of real(ity)—seen and unseen.

CHAPTER 7

sꜣḫw r sꜣḫw *and Evolutionary Genesis, Research, and the Science of Being*

A Summary

In dominant academic discourse, the Western Grand Narrative is often characterized by its emphasis on individualism, linear progress, universalism, and control over nature. It privileges nomological-deductive reasoning, a method that seeks to derive general laws from observable phenomena, and it utilizes quantitative and qualitative methodologies largely rooted in Cartesian dualism and empiricism. Knowledge production within this narrative is framed by a disconnection between the knower and the known, the object and the subject, and the spirit and the body.

As part of this summation, in *From Black Psychology to Sakhu Djaer: Implications for the Further Development of a Pan African Black Psychology* (Nobles, 2015a), I proposed that we formulate an African Grand Narrative based in *"Kmt–Nubia/BaNtu–Kongo"* thought that interrogates the knowing implications of the classical civilizations of Kmt (Egypt) and Nubia, and the ancient beliefs of the BaNtu and Kongo people. Such an African Grand Narrative posits that reality is "Spirit" and that a particular process of knowing emerges from African genesis or creation myths, meaning of being human, and concept of life and death. An African Grand Narrative would and should reflect and represent the voice of African people on the continent and throughout the diaspora.

The African-Centered Grand Narrative is one that emphasizes relationality, spirit-centeredness, and communal harmony. At its core lies the paradigm of the interconnected rings of personhood, familyhood, and neighborhood, with wellness residing at their concentric center. This model resists fragmentation and instead affirms wholeness, coherence, and continuity across all realms of reality—visible and invisible. The African worldview rests on several key ontological, epistemological, axiological, and teleological requirements where the Nature of Being (Ontology) is understood as spirit-first—dynamic, energetic, and multidimensional. Human beings are not isolated individuals but are seen as DEMM—entangled in cosmic, ancestral, and ecological networks. Life is a process of becoming rather than a fixed state, exemplified by the BaNtu–Kikongo concept of Zola–Ngolo, the spiraling force of love and vitality. Knowing and Knowledge (Episteme) is not acquired through abstraction or detachment but is relational, ritual-based, and ancestrally mediated. It is retrieved through remembering, a process of reconnection with ancestral memory, spiritual intuition, embodied experience, and oral transmission. Dreams, symbols, stories, and rhythm are not mere metaphors; they are epistemic tools. The goal and/or purpose of inquiry (Teleology) is not conquest or control, but the healing of disconnection and the activation of collective flourishing. Knowledge production is sacred and must uplift personhood, strengthen familyhood, and empower neighborhood/peoplehood. Axiologically (Value Orientation) Knowledge must serve the restoration of balance and dignity. It is not neutral or apolitical but is guided by ethical principles grounded in concepts that emphasize harmony, reciprocity, and justice.

One of the most profound distinctions between Western and African-centered thought lies in the acknowledgment and integration of multiple realms of reality. The African grand narrative affirms that life and knowledge operate simultaneously across the visible (material) and invisible (immaterial/spiritual) realms. These realms are not oppositional but seamless, interpenetrating dimensions of a unified cosmos. The visible realm includes physical matter, human bodies, material artifacts, institutions, observable phenomena, and quantifiable interactions. It is where daily life unfolds but is not the limit of existence. The invisible realm encompasses ancestral presence, spiritual forces, bioenergetic fields, dreams, intuition, memory, divine intention, and cosmic law. It is unseen but not unreal, and it is often the source from which events in the visible realm derive meaning, purpose, and direction (see comparison below).

COMPARISON OF WESTERN AND AFRICAN GRAND NARRATIVES

Dimension	Western Grand Narrative	African Grand Narrative
Ontological Basis	Dualistic: mind/body, spirit/matter, human/nature.	Unified: all reality is interconnected; being is spirit in relationship with others, nature, and cosmos.
Nature of the Self	Individualism: The self is autonomous, rational, and self-contained.	Relational Identity: The self exists within community—"I am because we are" (Ubuntu).
Epistemology (Knowing)	Nomological deductive reasoning: Knowledge comes through logic, empirical data, and abstraction.	Relational, embodied, and ancestral knowing: Knowledge comes through experience, ritual, intuition, and memory.
Reality	Materialist and secular: Only the visible world is considered real and valid.	Multi-dimensional: Visible and invisible realms are equally real and interdependent.
Time	Linear and progressive: Time moves forward; history is evolutionary.	Cyclical and ancestral: Time spirals through seasons, generations, and ancestral presence.

(Continued)

Dimension	Western Grand Narrative	African Grand Narrative
View of Nature	Nature is a resource to be studied, controlled, and used.	Nature is sacred, relational, and intelligent—a teacher and ancestor.
Teleological Purpose of Inquiry	To generate objective, generalizable knowledge for control and prediction.	To produce healing, restoration, and harmony within personhood, familyhood, and neighborhood.
Validation of Truth	Truth is universal, fixed, and validated through measurement and replicability.	Truth is contextual, dynamic, and validated through ancestral coherence, ritual, and lived moral harmony.
Methods of Knowing	Quantitative and experimental design; qualitative inquiry within positivist or constructivist limits.	Ritual, oral history, proverb, dream-time walking, Zaya Discourse, divination, dance, storytelling.
Sacred and Spiritual	Often excluded from research and theory.	Central to all knowledge production and social life; spirit is the first reality.
Language and Word Power	Language is a neutral tool for describing reality.	Language (Nommo) is creative, alive, and sacred—it activates and shapes reality.
Healing and Wellness	Illness is a biological or psychological condition to be treated mechanistically.	Healing is energetic and communal—involves restoring balance across realms of being.
Social Order	Hierarchical, individual-based; often competitive.	Cooperative, communal, intergenerational, and consensus-driven.
Memory and History	Memory is personal or archival. History is documented fact.	Memory is ancestral and lived, passed through oral tradition, ritual, and spirit possession.
Educational Emphasis	Focus on abstraction, categorization, and standardized testing.	Focus on embodiment, ritual learning, elder knowledge, and participatory experience.
Research Orientation	Researcher is detached observer; subjectivity is a flaw.	Researcher is a participant, often in communion with spirit, ancestors, and community.
Ultimate Aim	Control, progress, efficiency, mastery.	Balance, re-membering, harmony, and continuity—across people, nature, and cosmos.

African-centered epistemology insists that any valid understanding of a person, family, or community must engage both
realms. Illnesses, disruptions, and conflicts in the visible world
are understood as symptoms of disconnection or imbalance in
the invisible world—requiring ritual, remembrance, and spiritual coherence for restoration. The interconnected rings of
personhood, familyhood, and neighborhood are therefore not
merely social constructs but spiritual configurations that must
be harmonized across both realms. For instance, a person out
of alignment with ancestral guidance may experience psychological or spiritual fragmentation. A family that fails to uphold
ritual continuity may find itself vulnerable to generational
trauma. A neighborhood disconnected from land and cosmology
may suffer collective amnesia and systemic breakdown.

In this view, knowledge is not only cognitive but cosmic. The
Africana researcher, healer, or educator must cultivate the ability to
perceive, interpret, and act in both realms, often through processes
like ritual, dreaming, ancestral invocation, and symbolic engagement. The African-centered paradigm shifts the focus from the
individual to the communal spirit being-in-relation. Its distinctive
features include the following: (1) Primacy of Interconnectedness:
Being is interdependent. No person exists in isolation. The self is
only intelligible through relationships—with family, ancestors, the
community, the environment, and the cosmos; (2) Spiritness as
Essence: Humans are fundamentally spirit; the body is a temporary
container. Life is sacred because it is a manifestation of divine
energy; (3) identity is a social, communal, spirit-defined, and moral
construct formed in the context of one's responsibility to others;
(4) the visible and invisible realms must be in alignment. Disharmony
in one realm disrupts the other; and (5) to know is to heal. True
knowledge must mend brokenness, restore ancestral continuity,
and reweave the communal fabric.

To support these values and ontologies, Africana researchers should draw upon culturally congruent and spirit-defined grounded methods, such as Narrative and Ritual Inquiry, Zaya Discourse (Invocation–Revelation–Activation), Mbongi and Indaba Forums, Nommo-Based Inquiry (Word as Creative Force), Embodied Knowing (Drumming, Dance, Movement), Dream-Time Walking, and Ancestral Communication and Transgenerational Data Ethics (Data as Sacred Echoes). Each of these methods must acknowledge the dual presence of reality and the need to engage both realms responsibly and reverently.

This African-centered framework also posits that all research and inquiry should align with the interconnecting rings, structured as (1) Personhood: Focus on the cultivation of dignity, healing from disconnection, spirit alignment, and self-reclamation through ancestral awareness; (2) Familyhood: Investigate and strengthen intergenerational transmission of values, memory, rituals, and relational accountability; (3) Neighborhood/Peoplehood: Explore structures of communal resilience, cultural sovereignty, ecological stewardship, and Ubuntu-based governance; and (4) Core of Wellness defined not as mere absence of illness but as energetic, spiritual, communal, and moral balance across both the visible and invisible realms.

In summary, being as spirit is a radical African-centered research process of epistemic restoration that reclaims traditional African ways of knowing disrupted by colonial and Western incursions. Accordingly, it is especially important to be reminded that the traditional research language and overall process used here should be filtered through the paradigm shifting ideas of $s^i hw$ r $s^i hw$ and evolutionary genesis, spirit being (DEMM) and realms of reality. As such, African-centered research paradigm with coresearcher/respondents could be thought of as an information producing bubble that is multi-realms traversing the interconnected rings of wellness in personhood, familyhood, and neighborhood/peoplehood (see schema below).

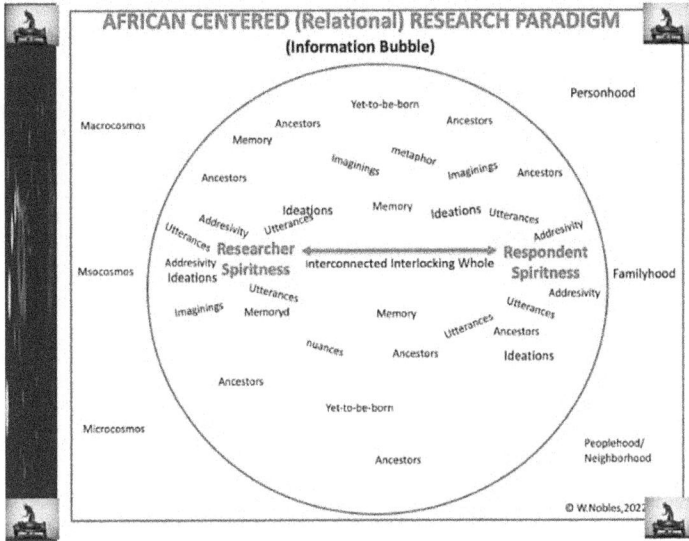

AFRICAN CENTERED (Relational) RESEARCH PARADIGM
(Information Bubble)

© W. Nobles, 202?

sᵌḥw r sᵌḥw and evolutionary genesis is coherent knowing and knowledge production grounded in the African worldview. It is the scientific and spirit-defined process of remembering who we are, where we come from, and how we co-create reality. This summary outlines *sᵌḥw r sᵌḥw* and evolutionary genesis as a coherent research process, including its ontological, epistemological, and axiological premises with implications for theory building, sample selection, data analysis, and validation.

The Ontological, Epistemological, and Axiological Premise	
Paradigm Question	**Evolutionary Genesis**
What is the nature of Being? (Ontology)	Being is Spirit—an energetic, multidimensional, ancestral presence manifesting as humans.
How is knowledge acquired? (Epistemology)	Through embodied experience, ancestral memory, bio-phonic resonance, and Zaya Discourse.
What is the role of values? (Axiology)	Centering Ubuntu, Kimuntu, Ma'at: values emerge from co-creation with ancestors, land, and cosmos.

Being is not static. It is spirit-defined becoming as a rhythmic spiral of emergence. Humans are DEMM, cocreating the cosmos through memory, ritual, and moral vibration.

Theory Construction: Theories rooted in spirit(ness) and DEMM challenge the foundational assumptions of conventional scientific thought. To build new theories that incorporate these concepts, one must begin with the premise that reality is not divided into neatly segregated physical and spirit-defined domains. Instead, human beings are viewed as dynamic spirit beings, interconnected with both the seen and unseen forces of the universe. This conceptualization aligns with the idea that spirit(ness) is not just a mental or psychological attribute but a fundamental component of the human experience that interacts with the material world in profound ways.

In theory construction, this approach expands the scope of research to include elements such as ancestral energy, spirit resonance, and the divine flow of energy as variables that shape human behavior, consciousness, and societal functioning. Theoretical frameworks based on spirit(ness) and DEMM might draw on indigenous African epistemologies, which emphasize interconnection, healing, and the cyclical nature of life. For instance, a theory could be constructed that views human behavior not as isolated actions but as an ongoing interaction between the physical self, ancestral spirits, and divine energies.

A new theory grounded in spirit(ness) and DEMM might also draw from quantum mechanics' ideas of entanglement and resonance, suggesting that individuals are "entangled" within a spirit-defined web of familial, community, and ancestral influences. This theory would, therefore, challenge the traditional, linear models of causality and propose a more fluid, dynamic interaction between the visible and invisible realms.

sꜣḥw r sꜣḥw and evolutionary genesis rejects Cartesian dualism. Theories must integrate the visible and invisible, material, and ancestral.

Key Components of Spirit-based Theory Construction:

- Reality as interwoven with ancestral energy and divine intent
- Behavior as influenced by both physical and spirit-defined environments
- Quantum concepts of entanglement and resonance as metaphors for community and memory

Spirit-defined resonance could be assessed using qualitative techniques such as ethnographic observations, focus groups, and personal reflections to understand how individuals or communities experience their connection to ancestral memory. At the same time, quantitative tools could measure variables such as mental health outcomes, community cohesion, or resilience to trauma, providing a dual lens of analysis.

Sample selection: In traditional research methods, sample selection is often based on a random or convenience sampling model, focusing on the physical attributes of the population. However, when conducting research grounded in spirit(ness) and DEMM, sample selection would need to reflect the interconnected nature of human existence. This means that the selection of participants would be informed by both their visible (physical) attributes and their spirit-defined or ancestral connections. In the methodological framework of *Evolutionary genesis*, sample selection should be spirit-defined and spirit-driven. It must encompass both the visible and invisible realms of reality. This dual-realm approach reflects the African cosmological understanding that reality is not solely defined by what is materially observable, but includes the spirit-defined, metaphysically attuned, and ancestrally guided dimensions that influence and shape human experiences. Sample selection within *sᵉḫw r sᵉḫw* and evolutionary genesis honors the African imperative to consult both the material and the metaphysical, both empirical relevance and spirit-defined resonance.

Criteria for sample selection: Sampling should be purposeful and energetic, guided by vibrational coherence and ancestral resonance, rather than randomization. It should be judged as both coherent and resonant. At minimum, the criteria for inclusion or selection should be persons with lived or inherited experiences of ancestral communication, bio-phonic healing, or spirit-defined memory recall; show evidence of spirit-driven and/or spirit-defined practices or traditions rooted in African cosmologies, and predictable "representations" across the interlocking rings of personhood, familyhood, and neighborhood.

Engaging two realms of reality: In the visible realm, sample selection mirrors conventional methods—identifying individuals, families, communities, or neighborhoods based on observable traits, characteristics, or conditions. This is what might be called the **"witness of form"**—those who bear evidence in the physical world of inherited or remembered cultural-spirit-defined continuity or disruption. In this realm, sample selection mirrors conventional methods—identifying individuals, families, communities, or neighborhoods based on observable traits, characteristics, or conditions. These may include sociocultural affiliations (e.g., African American, Afro-Brazilian, Wolof-speaking); behavioral patterns; historical location or geospatial significance; demographics (age, gender, etc.); and responses to spirit-defined or ancestral dislocation.

In the invisible realm, sample selection is not random nor merely intuitive. It is spirit-guided, memory-evoked, and resonance-attuned. African thought acknowledges that the "*Yet-to-Be*," the living, and the "*After-Living*," with the ancestral continuum communicating with, guiding, and influencing those in the material world. Thus, the dwellers in the invisible realm, ancestors, spirit-defined entities, unborn generations, and archetypal energies should be seen as informing who and what should be included in a sample for study. Sample selection is spirit-guided, memory-evoked, and resonance-attuned. African thought acknowledges that the "*Yet-to-Be*," the living, and the "*After-Living*," with the ancestral continuum communicating with, guiding, and influencing those in the material world. Thus, the dwellers in the invisible realm, ancestors, spirit-defined entities, unborn generations, and archetypal energies should be seen as informing who and what should be included in a sample for study.

The visible realm offers the terrain. The invisible realm offers the divine map. True research rooted in African knowing is not only about observing the world but about being called into it by the world beyond. Thus, the dwellers in the invisible realm are not passive ghosts of the past, but active selectors of who must speak, remember, and carry the flame forward. In this way, *sᶦḥw* r *sᶦḥw* and evolutionary genesis transcends sampling as simple selection. It becomes sampling as spirit-defined restoration. For instance, in a study on ancestral memory and spirit-defined healing, sample selection could involve selecting individuals who have demonstrated a deep connection to their ancestral heritage, such as through cultural practices, familial rituals, or spirit-defined practices. These individuals may be more attuned to the energies and ancestral wisdom that are central to the research. Additionally, sampling could extend to populations that are not only based on demographic factors such as race, age, and gender but also spirit-defined and psychological factors, including levels of attunement to ancestral memory or spirit-defined resonance.

Moreover, in studies related to community wellness or ancestral healing, a CBPR approach may be applied, where entire communities, rather than individuals alone, are included as study participants. This is because the collective energy of the community, the interconnections between persons, family, and neighborhood, and the ancestral influences that shape these communities are integral to understanding the whole.

Sample Selection Method and Reality Realms	
Realm	Method of Selection
Visible Realm	Observable traits: behavior, cultural practices, demographics, trauma markers
Invisible Realm	Spirit-guided resonance, ancestral appearance in dreams, oracular guidance, Zaya discourse

Criteria for inclusion:

- Demonstrated connection to ancestral or spirit-defined practices
- Experience of bio-phonic or ancestral communication
- Resonance with community and cosmological coherence

Invisible Realm Informs Sample Selection

- **Ancestral memory retrieval:** Individuals who experience dreams, visions, or inherited callings may be identified by the ancestors of those whose stories carry collective memory, trauma, or medicine. These individuals may not initially appear relevant from a traditional standpoint but are spirit-definedly "marked" as essential bearers of insight.
- **Bio-Phonic echoes:** Participants selected based on their resonance or sensitivity to bio-phonic communications—the spirit-defined "soundwaves" or impressions received through ritual, drumming, naming, or ancestral invocation—can be selected as carriers of invisible frequencies of knowledge.
- **Zaya discourse activation:** Sample selection may emerge through Zaya Discourse (dialogue between memory and imagination), where the researcher receives ancestral instruction, symbolic dreams, or intuitive recognitions of those who should be included in the inquiry.
- **Ritual and divination:** Traditional African sampling often includes consultation with oracles, diviners, or mediums, where spirit-defined technologies reveal who is cosmologically aligned to offer insight into a particular research question.
- **Case example:** In selecting participants for a study on intergenerational memory loss, for example, the Africana researcher would select African-ascendent participants, who have experienced loss of cultural knowledge, language, or family histories. Next through those in the invisible realm could be selected/contacted through libation, dream journaling, or divination, the researcher identifies three individuals whose ancestors have

"shown themselves" repeatedly in rituals, requesting their family story be told. The final sample includes not only those with visible trauma, but also those in the invisible with ancestral permission and spirit-defined resonance (carriers of untold stories necessary to *sᵎḥw r sᵎḥw* and evolutionary genesis).

Sample Research Agenda

The aim of this sample research agenda is to offer a preliminary sample for guiding the restorative coherence within the interconnecting rings of personhood, familyhood, and peoplehood with wellness located at their intersecting core.

Primary goals would be to (1) restore ancestral memory and spirit-defined coherence in African-ascended individuals and communities, (2) establish a culturally grounded methodology (Zaya Discourse) for research across metaphysical and material domains, (3) generate evidence-based practices for restoring personhood, familyhood, and peoplehood, and (4) engage Pan-African scholars and communities in quantum-informed, spirit-defined-grounded research.

Domains

Personhood: Spirit Being and Inner Coherence

- Identity formation, ancestral naming, internal coherence

Key questions:

- How does ancestral naming impact purpose realization?
- What role do dreams and inner visions play in affirming spirit-defined mission?
- Can entangled memory events predict spirit-defined misalignment or healing?

Familyhood: Ancestral Lineage and Generational Transmission

- Multigenerational healing, spirit-defined inheritance, collective dreaming:

Key questions:

- How do families experience shared ancestral visions or symbols?
- In what ways does Zaya Discourse repair generational ruptures caused by migration or enslavement?
- What spirit-defined rituals act as containers of intergenerational wisdom?

Peoplehood: Collective Memory and Cultural Purpose

- Diasporan cultural echoes, cross-continental ritual alignment, spirit-defined identity

Key questions:

- How do diasporan rituals reflect shared cosmologies across time and geography?
- What ancestral ethics are embedded in Africana art forms?
- Can Zaya Discourse reconstruct collective memory in post-genocidal or colonized communities?

Wellness at the Intersecting Core:

- Ma'atic harmony, and ecological and epistemological restoration

Key questions:

- What are the spirit-defined metrics of wellness in African-centered frameworks?
- How does quantum resonance affirm moral and energetic alignment?
- Can Zaya Discourse produce scalable healing interventions in community settings

Hypothesis Generation: Hypothesis generation should be grounded in Ancestral wisdom and energetic dynamics in the context of spirit(ness) and DEMM. Hypothesis generation should involve crafting research questions that consider the spirit-defined and energetic dimensions of human experience. Unlike traditional research, which often begins with hypotheses based on observable physical phenomena, hypotheses grounded in spirit(ness) and DEMM will focus on the unseen forces that influence human behavior and well-being. For example, a hypothesis might be framed as: "The alignment of individuals with ancestral memory and spirit-defined resonance will correlate with increased community wellness and personal healing outcomes." This hypothesis suggests that spirit-defined and ancestral connections are not peripheral to human experience but central to understanding psychological and social phenomena. Researchers may also hypothesize that astral resonance, the frequency at which individuals align with divine and ancestral energies, directly impacts their mental and physical health.

Another hypothesis could focus on entanglement: "Spirit-defined entanglement with ancestral and community energies enhances individual resilience in times of crisis, irrespective of material limitations." This hypothesis positions the invisible or spirit-defined realm as a fundamental source of strength that is linked to observable behaviors, suggesting that the entanglement of human spirits with the collective energy of community and ancestry can manifest in real-world benefits.

Data analysis: In Africana inquiry, knowledge is not solely derived from the material or visible domain but emerges in relation to the totality of being including the invisible, spirit(ness) realm. The methodology of *sᵢḥw* r *sᵢḥw* and evolutionary genesis defined as the process of rescuing, reclaiming, and refining African thought systems to guide contemporary inquiry demands that analysis engage with the full spectrum of African reality. In order to do this the research methodologist must repositioning analysis in *sᵢḥw* r *sᵢḥw* and evolutionary genesis.

Information (data) is not just derived from the material realm. It is not simply a set of observable phenomena. Information (data) should be thought of as a constellation of meanings, resonances, and spirit-guided revelations that unfold across biological, symbolic, ancestral, and energetic dimensions. Narratives from dreams, visions, oral histories, ancestral communication, and ritual enactments are all valid data. *The invisible is real and speaks.* Pieces of information (data) are energetic residues (*echoes*) that must be interpreted as spirit-defined and communally, not just statistically. They include the following: ritual artifacts, chants, songs, proverbs, transpersonal experiences, and ancestral visitations or spirit-defined promptings. Proposed data collection instruments could include oral narratives and transgenerational memory interviews, biophonic or dream journal documentation, energetic (via sound, movement vibration, heartbeat, tone) frequency/resonance mapping, and ancestral pattern tracing through rites, names, and family rituals.

The Africana research methodologist could create a data analytical fusion that represents and reflects $s^j\d{h}w$ r $s^j\d{h}w$ and evolutionary genesis *as* "Spirit coherence" by drawing upon traditional African cosmological logic. This could be defined or described as Spirit(ness) Coherency Analysis (SCA).

SCA is herein offered as a new culturally congruent African research method. SCA is spirit-defined spirit-driven technique that is theoretically designed to examine patterns of resonance, symbolic alignment, ancestral coherence, and cosmological significance across both realms of reality. It is guided by the understanding that both the information (data) and the Africana researcher are participants in a spirit-defined process of meaning-making driven by and reflecting the foundational catalytic episteme (see schema below).

Evolutionary Genesis
SCA Reflections Schema

Element of sᴵḥw r sᴵḥw and evolutionary genesis	Reflected in Spirit(ness) Coherency Analysis
Rescue	Restores ancient African analytical logics (e.g., Bantu-Kongo spiral logic, divinatory mapping).
Reclamation	Honors and reclaims symbolic, energetic, and metaphysical data as valid sources.
Refinement	Synthesizes traditional insight with contemporary research design in a spirit-definedly-coherent fashion.
DEMM and Spirit(ness) as Data Motifs	Treated as living, vibrating forces that shape, inform, and are revealed through data across both realms.

Conducting SCA: Prior to analysis, the researcher engages in an act of attunement, a spirit(ness) calibration that may include prayer, libation, drumming, meditation, or ancestral invocation. This prepares the participant to "see each other with spirit-defined eyes" and activate their spirit(ness) and enabling them to perceive non-material frequencies of meaning. Next, the information (data) would be coded (perceived) multidimensionally across three layers. Information (data) should be literally coding (capturing surface-level meaning), then energetically coding (assess emotional, vibrational, or spirit(ness)) charge. Finally identify metaphors, archetypes, ancestral motifs, or cosmological references.

The information (data): This layered approach symbolic coding allows the analyst to uncover DEMM expressions, instances where divine energy is made manifest through words, actions, or phenomena.

Information (data) is then examined for coherence mapping, the alignment between the participant's expressions and the cultural, ancestral, or cosmological truths embedded in African traditions. For instance, a repeated dream motif (e.g., crossing water) may be mapped onto Kongo cosmograms or Yoruba Ifá principles, revealing ancestral communication. Unlike statistical aggregation, SCA uses resonance patterning, identifying thematic or symbolic frequencies that recur across participants. This approach mirrors waveform logic—a principle found in both African cosmology and quantum physics—where meaning is not linear but vibrational and relational. The researcher then enters a reflexive dialogue and spirit-defined interpretation and relationship with the data, consulting elders, diviners, or spirit guides where appropriate—and interprets findings through a reverent, spirit-defined lens. Data interpretation is not reductionist, but reintegrative, reconnecting expressions to ancestral truths and community coherence.

Data Types Analyzed in Both Realms		
Realm	Data Expressions	Analytical Markers
Visible Realm	Interviews, surveys, behavioral observations, physiological data	Narrative coding, Likert scales, biophysical coherence
Invisible Realm	Dreams, symbols, ancestral messages, visions, bio-phonic waves, spirit dialog	Symbolic coding, resonance analysis, cosmological alignment

This *s³ḥw r s³ḥw* and evolutionary genesis analyses approach would or could evaluate patterns of meaning, resonance, and alignment across both material and immaterial expressions of data, privileging coherence with ancestral truths, symbolic messages, and energetic fields across realms of reality (see procedural steps below).

SPIRIT(NESS) COHERENCY ANALYSIS (SCA)

Procedural Steps

> **Step 1. Attunement:** Analyst undergoes a ritualized process (Zola–Ngolo, libation, or ancestral invocation) to attune their spirit and consciousness to multi-realm interpretation.

Reflects evolutionary genesis by activating spirit-informed knowing.

Step 2. Multidimensional coding: Information (data) are coded in layers:

- Surface meaning (material)
- Energetic charge (emotion/spirit)
- Symbolic/ancestral meaning (immaterial)

Step 3. Coherence mapping: Identifies alignment or misalignment between expressed data and ancestral/spirit-defined truths. For example, a narrative expressing "dislocation from purpose" may be coded both as psychological distress *and* as ancestral disconnection (a rupture in DEMM expression).

Step 4. Resonance patterning: Patterns are examined based on vibrational or thematic resonance, akin to waveform harmonics, rather than statistical generalization.

- For instance, multiple visions of fire across participants may be interpreted through ancestral symbology as transformative spirit-defined energy (Nganga fire).

Step 5. Reflexive dialogue: The analyst enters a reflective (sometimes ritualized) dialogue with the data, often invoking symbolic interpretation, ancestral guidance, or cosmological patterns (e.g., Dogon spiral, Kongo dikenga).

Step 6. Reverential interpretation: Interpretation is conducted reverently, with the understanding that both the analyst and the data are *participants in the unfolding of spirit(ness) and DEMM.*

Through Spirit(ness) Coherence Analysis, both information (data) types would be interpreted together. The lighting of a candle is not only a visible action but also resonates symbolically with "calling the light of DEMM." Dreams of ancestors are not seen as "subjective narratives" but as *valid data expressions* of spirit communication. Patterns of symbols (e.g., recurring birds, water, fire) could be mapped against African cosmologies for deeper interpretation. Consider in this regard that in our dreams form the truest expressions of our feelings and emotional beliefs about the world. Dream-time walking is believed to represent our ability via dreams to access the visible and the invisible realms of reality (with the invisible being far greater than the visible). The purpose of dreams is to process information, reflect the unconscious, aid in memory, reflect life experiences, prepare and protect, and process emotions. Theoretically, it is believed that through our nightly dreams and dream-time walking, we go back and forth from material to transitioning to immaterial from waking to sleeping (dream-time reality) until we touch (dance) the state beyond and embodiment the condition beyond this (reincarnation) to being light. A family's dream life or dream-time walking connects us to our ancestors and weaves us into the messages we send to our children's children. Dream-time walking should be thought of as an untapped and unlimited area for study and subsequent African-centered data analyses.

Africana research methodologists could also utilize mixed-methods approaches that combine quantitative and qualitative techniques not as separate methods but as techniques that flow into and support each other. Qualitative data could include interviews, life histories, and spirit-defined experiences related to ancestral memory, while quantitative data might capture changes in health, wellness, and behavior through physiological measures, psychological assessments, and community engagement surveys. Spirit resonance could be assessed using qualitative techniques such as ethnographic observations, focus groups, and personal reflections to understand how individuals or communities experience their connection to ancestral memory. At the same time, quantitative tools could measure variables such as mental health outcomes, community cohesion, or resilience to trauma, providing a dual lens of analysis.

Information (data) results: Interpreting information (data) results derived from research on spirit(ness) and DEMM requires an approach that integrates both the visible and invisible realms. This means interpreting quantitative data in conjunction with qualitative insights into the participants' spirit-defined experiences, emotional responses, and cultural practices. The insights gained from studying ancestral memory, astral resonance, and entanglement may reveal complex interconnections between physical health, spirit-defined well-being, and social engagement that are not easily measurable through conventional scientific paradigms.

For instance, the interpretation of information (data) might reveal that individuals with stronger ancestral connections or higher levels of spirit-defined resonance exhibit greater psychological resilience or experience improved health outcomes following trauma or illness. The influence of entanglement, the interconnectedness of individuals with their communities and ancestors—might be seen in how spirit-defined practices, such as ritual and prayer create observable shifts in collective well-being.

The analysis of information (data) incorporates both qualitative and energetic modalities. African researchers should consider the following techniques: (1) Narrative Analysis—focused on ancestral motifs, symbols, and themes; (2) Symbolic Resonance Analysis— mapping sound, name, or color frequencies to ancestral traditions; (3) Pattern Recognition—tracking recurring cosmological structures (triads, spirals, circles) in participant stories; and (4) Astral Data Coding—interpreting dreams, visions, or spirit visitations as coded information systems.

Traditional empirical analysis, constrained by positivist assumptions and reductive coding schemas that cannot adequately capture the presence of spirit(ness) (the animating essence of life) or DEMM—the realization of divinity within human experience. Thus, a new method of analysis must emerge: one that is Spirit coherent, cosmologically aligned, and epistemologically grounded in African ways of knowing.

Analysis therefore should be dialogic and layered. It could even be done through the interplay of memory and imagination *(Zaya Discourse)*, through symbolic, metaphoric, and rhythmic modes of interpretation that honor ancestral and spirit-defined dimensions. To analyze data within the context of spirit(ness) and DEMM, researchers could also utilize approaches that combine quantitative and qualitative techniques. Qualitative data could include interviews, life histories, and spirit-defined experiences related to ancestral memory, while quantitative information (data) might capture changes in health, wellness, and behavior through physiological measures, psychological assessments, and community engagement surveys. Researchers might also turn to bioenergetics and bio-photonics, which allow for the measurement of energy patterns within the human body. These tools could help quantify the "spirit-defined energy" or resonance that participants emit and how this aligns with their perceived connection to ancestral and divine energies. Data on astral resonance, energy fields, and changes in spirit-defined attunement might be gathered using tools such as electroencephalogram (EEG) readings or HRV, linking spirit-defined dynamics to physical health outcomes.

To analyze information (data) within the context of spirit(ness) and DEMM, Africana researchers are invited to explore and even invent culturally congruent analytical approaches grounded in *sᵌḥw r sᵌḥw* and evolutionary genesis. In the context of *sᵌḥw r sᵌḥw* and evolutionary genesis grounded in the *rescue, reclamation, and refinement* of African epistemologies to guide contemporary knowing, the data analytical approach must *necessarily* account for both the visible (material) and invisible (immaterial) realms of reality. When the phenomena under investigation are, for instance, spirit(ness) (the essential, animating force of being) and DEMM conventional analytical frameworks are insufficient. Instead, an integrative analytical approach that centers *ancestral logic, coherence, resonance, symbolic meaning, and* methodological fusion is needed.

African-centered research methodologists might also turn to bio-energetics and bio-photonics, which allow for the measurement of energy patterns within the human body. These tools could help quantify the "spirit-defined energy" or resonance that participants emit and how this aligns with their perceived connection to ancestral and divine energies. Data on astral resonance, energy fields, and changes in spirit-defined attunement might be gathered using tools such as electroencephalogram (EEG) readings or HRV, linking spirit-defined and spirit-driven dynamics to physical health outcomes.

The idea that *"We are spirit beings housed in a physical container having a human experience"* also resonates deeply across major frameworks of Black psychological thought. This central tenet reflects a foundational African worldview that conceives of the human being as fundamentally spirit in essence, material in manifestation, and relational in function.

Across these frameworks, major Black psychologists emphasize that African people are spirit beings first, and that psychological wellness, identity, and liberation begin with the reclamation of the spirit-defined self is congruent with traditional African epistemic reflections.

The phrase "We are spirit beings housed in a physical container having a human experience" is not only affirmed by evolutionary genesis but is further elaborated through Black psychology's call for realignment with African cosmological traditions.

Validation and reliability: *sᶦḫw r sᶦḫw* and evolutionary genesis recognize that data appear not only in visible form, words, behaviors, physiological responses but also in invisible manifestations such as dreams, synchronicities, symbolic visions, ancestral visitations, and energetic disturbances. These data types are equally valid and must be interpreted using culturally and spirit-defined and spirit-driven appropriate methods. Spirit(ness)-coherence analysis expands the scope and depth of what constitutes "data" and how it is interpreted, particularly within African-centered research, cosmology, and restoration traditions. It affirms that meaning resides not only in words but in vibrations, dreams, symbols, silences, and energies, that is, the total expression of Spirit(ness). Through this methodology, *sꜣḫw r sꜣḫw* and evolutionary genesis are realized as a living epistemic act: a return to wholeness, to coherence, and to divine knowing through DEMM. Accordingly, Africana research methodologists are encouraged to invent and create new and unique methods for defining data (information) and analyses. In this vein, I want to offer, as example, the idea of a spirit(ness) coherent analytical plan. Findings are considered valid not through replication but through *resonance*—when they reverberate with ancestral truths, align with community wisdom, and spark healing found in community interpretation circles, congruency with historical, linguistic, and cosmological knowledge, and repetition or confirmation across multiple realms (dreams, rituals, behavior, and spoken words).

Population of study: Traditional research categorizes participants by demographics. *sꜣḫw r sꜣḫw* and evolutionary genesis are selected based on spirit-defined coherence and ancestral resonance.

Following are the examples of DEMM subjects:

- Children exhibiting ancestral knowledge
- Adults awakened by dream visitations
- Elders whose wisdom resonates with cosmic patterns
- Families practicing intergenerational naming or ritual

Spirit(ness) coherency analysis (SCA): SCA is a methodology of analysis that centers ancestral, energetic, and cosmological logic. It is both rigorous and reverent.

PROCEDURAL STEPS OF SPIRIT(NESS) COHERENCY ANALYSIS

1. Attunement: Ritual invocation (libation, drumming, meditation)
2. Multidimensional coding:
   o Literal: Surface meanings
   o Energetic: Emotional/spiritual charge
   o Symbolic: Cosmological/ancestral themes
3. Coherence mapping: Alignment with ancestral truths
4. Resonance patterning: Nonlinear harmonics and vibrations across data
5. Reflexive dialogue: Ancestral and community interpretive input
6. Reverential interpretation: Final analysis guided by cosmological and community alignment

Realm Data Type and Analysis Method		
Realm	Data Type	Analysis Method
Visible Realm	Surveys, interviews, behavior physiology	Coding, correlation, thematic analysis
Invisible Realm	Dreams, rituals, visions, bio-phonic signals	Symbolic resonance, Zaya discourse

Sample Research Agenda and Questions		
Ring of Inquiry	Sample Topic	Key 1 Investigatory Questions
Personhood	Ancestral Naming & Identity	How does naming influence purpose? What dreams affirm spirit-defined mission?
Familyhood	Multigenerational Ritual Healing	How does Zaya Discourse restore intergenerational rupture?
Peoplehood	Diasporan Ritual Echoes	How do rituals reflect cosmological coherence across geography?
Wellness Core	Spirit-defined Metrics of Wellness	What are measurable effects of ritual on mental-emotional alignment?

Data Collection Instruments:

- Oral narratives and memory interviews
- Dream journaling and symbolic content analysis
- Bio-phonic resonance mapping (sound, tone, heartbeat)
- Ritual observation, libation documentation, altar symbolism
- Energetic patterning tools (e.g., HRV, EEG)

Interpretation: In Seeing With Spirit-Defined Eyes interpretation requires integrating:

- Community wisdom and ancestral input
- Cross-realm pattern recognition (e.g., cosmograms, dreams, chants)
- Non-reductive frameworks grounded in rhythm, spiral, and resonance

Validation and reliability: *sꜣḥw r sꜣḥw* and evolutionary genesis are achieved not through replication, but resonance:

- Confirmation across dreams, rituals, and material outcomes
- Alignment with historical, cosmological, and ancestral truths
- Community interpretation and healing activation

sꜣḥw r sꜣḥw **and evolutionary genesis as coherent knowing:** *sꜣḥw r sꜣḥw* and evolutionary genesis transform research into a sacred act. Knowing becomes an unfolding memory, an echo of the ancestors. Through spirit(ness), through DEMM, through rhythm and resonance, we do not simply study reality. We co-create it. Researchers are not extractors but restorers. This methodology offers a template for reclaiming African wisdom, refining modern inquiry, and restoring cosmic coherence.

Four Case Study Areas		
Case Study Area	Realm-Based Methods	Expected Outcome
Intergenerational Memory & Communication	Dreams, songs, ancestral rituals (Zaya discourse + interviews)	Patterned themes, blocked energy revealed, restorative family rituals
Sound, Vibration & Healing (Zola Mpasi)	Drumming, HRV, trance experiences	Restoration typologies, ancestral rhythm categories
Naming & Identity	Initiation names, pre/post analysis, dream tracking	Typology of cosmological roles, identity alignment scales
Ritual Technologies for Healing IGSH	Ritual space design, song, libation, guided visualization	Ritual toolkit, measurable increase in spirit-defined clarity and wellness

Suggested Future Research Areas

- Quantum Entanglement & Spirit Communication
- Diasporan Ritual Synchrony Across Continents
- Healing through Collective Dreaming Practices
- Ancestral Memory Recovery in Communities Displaced by Genocide

sᵢḥw r *sᵢḥw* and evolutionary genesis are the return to a coherent knowing. The light of DEMM shines where remembering, ritual, and research become one.

Population core: All African-ascended peoples, and by extension all human beings, are considered DEMM—spirit beings manifest in physical form, each carrying a mission, memory, and energy encoded in their being. The African personhood is not separate from the divine. It is divine with **spirit-defined consciousness;** seeking experience or transmission of ancestral memory; and alignments or misalignments across personhood, familyhood, and neighborhood.

An expanded listing of population characteristics can be interrogated below.

Key Population Characteristics	
Characteristic	Description
Spirit-Nature (Essence)	Each participant is more than their flesh and is defined by their internal, divine spark
Cosmic Purpose	Life is lived not randomly but as part of a cosmological unfolding; each person has a role
Cultural Grounding	Participants may or may not be consciously grounded in African worldviews, but are spirit-defined connected through ancestral codes.
Trauma Imprints	Many DEMM beings carry intergenerational harm or psychic dislocation due to colonialism, slavery, or disconnection
Healing Capacity	Through rituals, memory work, and restoration, DEMM beings can realign with their essence
Vibrational Awareness	Capacity for spirit-defined attunement and engagement with invisible signals through dreams, vision, or intuitive alignment.

Examples of DEMM as a population:

- Children who exhibit ancestral knowledge or abilities without being taught
- Adults undergoing spirit reawakening through dream visitations
- Families who practice intergenerational naming and rituals
- Elders whose wisdom holds cosmological coherence
- Communities who sustain spirit-defined-cultural ecosystems of practice (e.g., drumming, libation, initiation rites)

SUGGESTED COHERENCY RESEARCH AREAS AND INVESTIGATORY QUESTIONS

In any preliminary exploration of $s^i\underline{h}w \ r \ s^i\underline{h}w$ and evolutionary genesis methodology, it is recommended that researcher locate their research initiatives as an act of restoration rather than extraction. It should seek understanding as the rebalancing of frequencies across time and space. Ultimately, it is a praxis enterprise that involves cocreating the activation of DEMM. Suggested research areas could include shattered consciousness and fractured identity formation through mending and ancestral naming through spirit-defined invocation; Dream recall and ancestral memory as sources of purpose; intergenerational trauma, psychic terrorism, and vibrational dissonance; and bio-phonic resonance and internal healing practices.

Research areas: Research areas would include investigating diasporan cultural expressions as echoes of ancestral cosmologies (e.g., jazz, gospel, capoeira, vodun); cross-continental spirit-defined coherence (ritual simultaneity, shared feast days, drum language); Africana epistemologies of healing and justice; quantum entanglement and collective resonance across geographies; spirit-defined inheritance through family rituals, music, and symbols; collective dreaming and intergenerational communication; disruption and restoration of family rituals (e.g., libation, storytelling, drumming); family-based healing circles and cosmological coherence; familyhood, ancestral lineage and types of generational transmission; diasporan spirit-defined traditions reflect the ontological unity of African cosmologies; cosmological patterns found in diasporan music, ritual, or dance that link back to specific African ethnic groups; Zaya Discourse used to reconstruct cultural memory in communities affected by genocide, colonization, or displacement; in what ways does quantum entanglement mirror African understandings of spirit communication across time and space?

Investigatory questions: Investigatory questions could address how African-ascended persons, families and communities retrieve and interpret ancestral memory through informal and formal Black study as well as dreams or inner visions; what role does ancestral naming play in affirming identity and destiny; how does imagination and memory (Zaya Discourse) support spirit-defined reintegration in persons experiencing psychic fragmentation or dissociation; and can entangled memory patterns across siblings or cousins be traced through symbolic dreams and rituals across realms of reality; how are spirit-defined memories passed down through maternal or paternal lines in diasporan families; in what ways do families experience "entangled healing" through shared spirit-defined practices; how does imagination and memory (Zaya Discourse) facilitate multigenerational meaning-making in families disrupted by migration, slavery, or displacement?; what symbols, objects, or oral traditions act as carriers of ancestral energy in African-ascended families.

PEOPLEHOOD: COLLECTIVE MEMORY, CULTURE, AND PURPOSE

Wellness at the Intersecting Core

Research Areas: Epistemological, Ecological, and Moral Harmony

- Wellness as coherence across visible and invisible realms
- Restoration of balance using ancestral ethics and vibrational realignment
- Epistemological restoration through ancestral knowledge systems
- Interventions rooted in ancestral ecology, harmony, and moral order (Ma'at)

Investigatory questions:

- What are the measurable effects of ancestral ritual on psychological and emotional wellness?
- How can Zaya Discourse inform clinical practices for African-ascended populations?
- In what ways does alignment with ancestral energy improve self-regulation and spirit-defined integrity?
- How does the restoration of personhood–familyhood–peoplehood through spirit-defined praxis affect community well-being?

Interpretation: Integrating the Visible and Invisible Realms

Interpreting data derived from research on spirit(ness) and DEMM requires an approach that integrates both the visible and invisible realms. This means interpreting quantitative data in conjunction with qualitative insights into the participants' spirit-defined experiences, emotional responses, and cultural practices. The insights gained from studying ancestral memory, astral resonance, and entanglement may reveal complex interconnections between physical health, spirit-defined well-being, and social engagement that are not easily measurable through conventional scientific paradigms.

For instance, the interpretation of data might reveal that individuals with stronger ancestral connections or higher levels of spirit-defined resonance exhibit greater psychological resilience or experience improved health outcomes following trauma or illness. The influence of entanglement, the interconnectedness of individuals with their communities and ancestors, might be seen in how spirit-defined practices, such as ritual and prayer, create observable shifts in collective well-being.

FOUR SPECIFIC EXAMPLES FOR AFRICANA METHODOLOGISTS

Study Area 1: Intergenerational Memory and Ancestral Communication

Possible research question: How do African-ascended communities engage in bio-phonic ancestral communication through ritual, song, and dream to restore disrupted personhood?

Visible Realm Data Sources:

- Ethnographic observation of ritual (e.g., libation, ancestral altars).
- Interviews on dreams, visions, or ancestor visitations.
- Archival analysis of praise songs, death announcements, or spirit-defined testimonies.

Invisible realm investigation:

- Zaya Discourse method to access ancestral memory through guided journaling and meditative drumming.
- Spirit-medium communication or dream analysis led by traditional healer.
- Divination (Ifá, Dikenga reading, or throwing bones) to identify intergenerational wounds or missed ancestral contracts.

Probable outcome:

- A mapped pattern of ancestral themes across generations (e.g., healer callings, migration disruptions).
- Identification of "blocked" ancestral energy (TDS—traumatized disconnected spirit).
- Co-created restorative ritual to reestablish personhood and DEMM alignment.

Study Area 2: Sound, Vibration, and Energetic Healing (Zola Mpasi)

Possible research question: How does African drumming as energetic intervention impact emotional and physiological regulation among displaced African-ascended populations?

Visible realm data sources:

- Physiological indicators (e.g., heart rate, cortisol).
- Participant interviews post-drum sessions.
- Behavioral observations (e.g., expression, posture, vocalizations).

Invisible realm exploration:

- Invoke Zola–Ngolo: measuring shifts in "verve" (life force) through narrative inquiry and dream journaling.
- Use call-and-response affirmations during sessions to track resonance with ancestral themes.

- Structured interviews exploring "spirit shifts" or trance experiences post-drumming.

Probable outcome:

- African-physiological map of wellness states activated by sonic healing.
- Emergent categories for "restorative rhythms" unique to diasporic groups.
- Linkage of somatic restoration to ancestral resonance patterns.

Study Area 3: Naming, Identity, and DEMM (Spirit as Real Identity)

Possible research question: What is the relationship between spirit-defined naming practices and psychological alignment with African identity and cosmology?

Visible realm data sources:

- Case studies of individuals renamed through initiation, marriage, or self-reclamation.
- Content analysis of African and diasporan naming ceremonies.
- Interviews on pre- and post-naming identity shifts.

Invisible realm exploration:

- Engage in Zaya Discourse to uncover the spirit-defined calling of the name (name as vibration, contract, or destiny marker).
- Dream tracking: dreams before and after receiving the spirit-defined name.
- Ritual invocation of name in ceremony to detect energetic activation or coherence.

Probable outcome:

- Typologies of spirit-defined names linked to cosmological roles (e.g., *Nganga, Oba, Dibulu*).

- Development of an African-centered naming assessment tool that correlates names with DEMM expressions.
- New criteria for wellness and alignment tied to spirit-defined naming.

Study Area 4: Restorative Ritual Technologies for Healing IGSH (Intergenerational Sensoria-Harm)

Possible research question:

- How do community-based rituals informed by African cosmology mend spirit-defined disconnection from ancestral, ecological, and linguistic roots?

Visible realm data sources:

- Participatory documentation of ritual stages (song, dress, space layout, offerings).
- Pre-/post-ritual self-report scales of well-being or spirit-defined clarity.
- Symbolic analysis of altar objects or ritual gestures.

Invisible realm exploration:

- Guided visualizations for reconnecting with ancestral languages or lands (e.g., dreams spoken in unknown tongues).
- Tracking epigenetic memories activated during ritual (e.g., spontaneous weeping, tremors, ancestral speech).
- Analysis of ritual space as portal or liminal zone via soundscape and spatial design.

Probable outcome:

- A framework for ritual stages as therapeutic stages of reconnection.
- Classifications of ritual elements based on DEMM expressions.
- Development of "Ritual as Method" toolkit for African-centered clinical restoration.

CHAPTER 8
Rethinking Insanity
A BaNtu View

Across indigenous African peoples, including BaNtu/Kongo epistemology, being (or existence) is holistic and relational. A person's essence is understood not in isolated terms but through the interplay of cosmic forces, ancestral guidance, and community obligations. Spirit-defined disturbance is thus not *only* individual pathology but a sign of disharmony among broader relational networks (family, lineage, ancestors, and the divine cosmos).

In the BaNtu/Kongo worldview, the human spirit (or *moyo*) must remain in balanced relationship with the cosmic or ancestral plane (*kalunga*). Disruption in that relationship—through defilement of spirit or violation of communal/ancestral norms—can manifest as what the West might label "mental illness." However, from an African perspective, the cause is not solely in the psyche; it is simultaneously *spirit-defined*, *social*, and *cosmic*.

From a BaNtu/Kongo and broader African-centered perspective, "insanity" encompasses much more than an individual's mental symptoms. It is indicative of disruptions in spirit-defined, familial, and communal bonds, often traced to deeper historical and cosmic imbalances. Terms such as *Eni Orí ẹ Kòpé, Elenini, Kizungu Zungu,* and *Ukufa Kwabantu* highlight the ways in which African philosophies perceive mental instability as the fragmentation of consciousness and identity that arises when sacred, social, and cosmic orders are out of alignment.

In many African cosmological and philosophical traditions, human well-being is inseparable from spirit-defined, communal, and cosmic balance. Within BaNtu/Kongo thought in particular, broader African epistemologies such as Yoruba worldview "insanity" can be understood not merely as a biomedical or psychological phenomenon, but as a disruption or distortion of one's spirit-defined-communal integrity. In rethinking insanity, this essay as provocatory examines the concept of "insanity" (or mental imbalance) as articulated by terms such as *Eni Orí ẹ Kòpé* ("He who is unable to put his mind together," Yoruba), *Elenini* ("Spirit defilement," KiKongo), and *Kizungu Zungu* ("the defiled or damaged spirits [individual or collective]," often interpreted as "tornadoes of the mind" or "mental chaos"). We also **explore** *Ukufa Kwabantu* ("the disease of [African] people"), placing these ideas in dialogue with the notion of "shattered consciousness" and "fractured identity," as well as his framework of the interconnected rings of wellness. Ultimately, this discussion foregrounds the African-centered understanding that personal, familial, communal, and cosmic well-being form concentric circles, with "health" residing at the overlapping core.

KEY TERMINOLOGIES OF "INSANITY" OR MENTAL CHAOS

In Yoruba thought, *Eni Orí ẹ Kòpé* literally translates as "the person whose head (or mind) is not assembled or put together." The Yoruba concept of *orí* (head) includes not just the physical head, but the spirit-defined essence or destiny that each person carries into the world (Oladipo, 1992, p. 48). When one's *orí* is misaligned or defiled—whether through personal wrongdoing, ancestral neglect, or societal disharmony. This results in a distorted consciousness. Thus, "insanity" arises when the spirit-defined seat of consciousness is scattered rather than integrated.

In KiKongo, *Elenini* (often glossed as "spirit defilement") captures the idea that an impurity or contamination has entered one's spirit. This impurity is not simply an abstract notion; it can be caused by interpersonal conflict, broken taboos, or malevolent forces (Kagame, 1976, p. 23). It is a state of disequilibrium that can evoke anger, fear, or deep confusion—often experienced as both emotional and cognitive turmoil. *Kizungu Zungu* ("Tornadoes of the Mind") is often explained as "the defiled or damaged spirits" (individual or collective). *Kizungu Zungu* evokes a swirling chaos—akin to tornadoes—that uproot the stable center of a person's being. The term implies that mental disturbance involves multiple layers of turmoil (personal, ancestral, communal) colliding at once, leaving the sufferer disoriented or disconnected. This resonates with the BaNtu emphasis on *ngolo* (vital force) being out of balance (Janzen, 1982, p. 57).

In many Southern African contexts, *Ukufa Kwabantu* refers to an illness peculiar to the African socio-spirit-defined fabric. It underscores how historical traumas—colonialism, enslavement, forced migrations—have collectively wounded African people, producing both personal and communal disease. Mental disturbances such as Ukufa Kwabantu often stem from cumulative injuries that disrupt ancestral connections, lineage continuity, and cultural identity (Bynum, 2012, p. 132).

The concept of "shattered consciousness" and "fractured identity," alongside the model of the interconnected rings of wellness, illuminates these ideas. Evolutionary genesis *Skh* research, therefore, involves more than clinical intervention; it calls for a process of ritual reconnection, ancestral communion, and holistic communal support. Within this BaNtu/Kongo (African-centered) philosophical framework, sanity is ultimately the harmonious integration of the self's physical, spirit-defined, familial, and communal dimensions, a recentering of the person at the heart of overlapping circles of well-being, guided by a cosmic sense of order and moral responsibility.

In African-centered psychology, the idea of a "shattered consciousness" and "fractured identity" (Nobles, 2006, pp. 60–65) is generative. Within a Eurocentric paradigm, mental illness is frequently pathologized at the level of the individual's psyche. In contrast, the evolutionary genesis approach allows for the consideration of how oppressive social conditions—particularly those experienced by African-ascended populations—may "shatter" the collective consciousness. This fracturing leaves individual's spirit-defined, mentally, and communally disconnected.

In this regard, we have also proposed the idea of interconnecting rings of personhood, familyhood, and neighborhood where one ring constitutes personhood: the individual's spirit, personality, and sense of self. The second ring, familyhood, the core unit of social and cultural continuity, includes the living family, ancestors, and extended kin network, and the third ring, neighborhood or peoplehood, represents broader social structures, cultural norms, and supportive networks.

Wellness (in this model) resides at the overlapping center of these circles. Any disruption, for example, shattered consciousness and fractured identity, in one circle reverberates through the others (Nobles, 2015a, p. 89). Thus, if a person suffers from "insanity," it implies a misalignment rippling outward (and inward) across the family and communal rings.

When we link concept of a shattered consciousness to *Kizungu Zungu* ("tornadoes of the mind"), we see that the "tornado" can be viewed as the swirling chaos borne of historical dislocation, broken kinship ties, or existential wounding. "Shattered consciousness" highlights how personal psychic pain cannot be separated from communal or ancestral pain. The defilement or "damage" to the spirit—*Elenini*—manifests as a deep fragmentation throughout one's identity rings.

Healing, Restoration, and the Science of Being

In many African healing systems (Yoruba, Kongo, Zulu, etc.), the first step toward restoring sanity or wellness is *ritual reconnection*—with ancestors, with community, and with the self's divinely ordained path (orí, moyo). Ceremonies, prayer, offerings, and communal gatherings may be essential for cleansing spirit-defined defilements and reweaving fractured communal bonds (Somé, 1998, pp. 101–105).

MOVEMENT FROM BLACK PSYCHOLOGY TO THE SCIENCE OF BEING

I have advocated for an African-centered psychology that is not simply a variant of Western models but a *Science of Being* rooted in African cosmological principles (Nobles, 2006, pp. 66–70). This science recognizes that human beings are both *spirit being* and *social* and that "illness" and "health" cannot be reduced to the individual brain or mind but must be understood in communal, ancestral, and cosmological contexts; and asserts that the restoration of wellness involves the reclamation of African spirit-defined identity, and the reestablishing alignment among the concentric circles of personhood, familyhood, and neighborhood.

In alignment with *sꜣḥw r sꜣḥw* and evolutionary genesis, research driven by an African-centered paradigm, will regain wholeness as a means of counteracting the fragmentation of consciousness with "spirit remembering." *Eni Orí ẹ Kòpé* moves toward *Eni Orí ẹ Kapé* ("He whose mind is rightly put together") via a re-grounding in African culture, collective memory, and spirit-definedly guided moral-communal principles. This is where "interconnected rings of wellness" converge at the center, restoring equilibrium to the self, family, and community simultaneously.

Zaya, Ngolo, and Living Light together form a bioenergetic and quantum-based ancestral technology, ensuring that wisdom, energy, and presence remain accessible to future generations. Just as quantum mechanics explores non-locality and entanglement, BaNtu cosmology insists that ancestral energy is neither lost nor confined to linear time—it simply transforms and returns. The concept of Living Light supports the idea that all existence is embedded with intelligent, vibrational signatures that are transmittable across realms. *Zaya* is activated by *Ngolo*, ensuring that ancestral knowledge and spirit-defined energy continue to shape the present and future of its lineage. Thus, bio-phonic communication is not merely a method of knowing but a way of being—an affirmation that the echo of existence, once set in motion, never ceases to vibrate through space and time.

This discussion of insanity is offered to instigate future possibilities with research that may provide both new interpretations of insanity and African-centered research that not only produces knowing and knowledge production but simultaneously restores wellness.

CHAPTER 9
The Intellectual Continuum

In fact, the intellectual heritage of Africana and Africology scholars is marked by two critical methodological orientations: that I have identified as paradigm shifting and evolutionary genesis. Paradigm shifting refers to the radical reorientation of inquiry that challenges and displaces Eurocentric frameworks, while the traditional research language and overall process should be filtered through the paradigm shifting ideas of *sᵢḥw r sᵢḥw* and evolutionary genesis, spirit being (DEMM), and realms of reality. Almost all Africana researchers and scholars involve the reclamation, refinement, and reactivation of ancestral African knowledge systems as the genesis for new research, theory, and practice. Spanning over a century, Africana/Africology scholars and intellectuals have exemplified a sterling legacy of paradigm disruption and epistemic rebirth. Together, their work constitutes an evolving methodology for Africana and Africology, one that is rooted in ancestral memory, spirit, and sovereignty. The accompanying timeline visualizes not merely a sequence of historical contributions but a spirit-defined and intellectual continuum of liberation and restoration, a true $s^i\underline{h}w\ r\ s^i\underline{h}w$ and evolutionary genesis of African knowledge and vision.

This essay profiles twenty leading Africana scholars, identifying how each demonstrates paradigm shifting in their research orientation and applies $s^i\underline{h}w\ r\ s^i\underline{h}w$ and evolutionary genesis as a methodological foundation for African-centered knowledge construction. From W.E.B. Du Bois to my own contributions, each scholar's intellectual trajectories can be revisited and highlighted relative to $s^i\underline{h}w\ r\ s^i\underline{h}w$ and evolutionary genesis and paradigm shifting. Their work has contributed to the dynamic construction of Africana knowledge through this dual catalytic praxis with $s^i\underline{h}w\ r\ s^i\underline{h}w$ and evolutionary genesis. These contributions served and is serving not only to deconstruct colonial systems of thought but to activate the ancestral, metaphysical, and cultural wellsprings of African civilizations.

Readers are asked to review and visit the following scholar/intellectuals or add additional ones of your own choice.

W.E.B. DU BOIS—*THE SOULS OF BLACK FOLK* (1903)

Paradigm Shifting: Du Bois transformed sociological thought by introducing the concept of double consciousness, which challenged the dominant narrative of racial determinism and invited a deeper exploration of the lived Black experience in America.

$s^i\underline{h}w\ r\ s^i\underline{h}w$ and Evolutionary Genesis: He employed Pan-African frameworks and empirical research methodologies grounded in communal memory and African cultural values, laying the foundation for African American intellectual sovereignty.

FRANTZ FANON—*BLACK SKIN, WHITE MASKS* (1952)

Paradigm Shifting: Fanon revolutionized psychiatry and political theory by exposing the psychological trauma of colonialism and the necessity of revolutionary violence for psychic and political liberation.

sꜣḥw r sꜣḥw and Evolutionary Genesis: He synthesized ancestral memory and existential freedom, merging personal and cultural liberation into a methodology that connected healing with collective struggle.

KWAME NKRUMAH—*CONSCIENCISM* (1964)

Paradigm Shifting: Nkrumah articulated an African-centered philosophical foundation for political theory, resisting capitalist and Marxist paradigms that excluded African metaphysics.

sꜣḥw r sꜣḥw and Evolutionary Genesis: His methodology drew from traditional African communalism and spirit-defined values to articulate an authentically African ideological vision for national sovereignty and self-governance.

AYI KWEI ARMAH—*TWO THOUSAND SEASONS* (1973)

Paradigm Shifting: Armah rejected colonial historiography and linear time constructs by reclaiming African temporality, ethics, and communal values through epic narrative.

sꜣḥw r sꜣḥw and Evolutionary Genesis: He employed oral tradition and symbolic cosmology to reconstruct a restorative African future grounded in ancestral memory and metaphysical integrity.

AMÍLCAR CABRAL—*RETURN TO THE SOURCE* (1973)

Paradigm Shifting: Cabral linked cultural identity directly to political liberation, emphasizing culture as a revolutionary tool for dismantling colonial structures.

sᶦḥw r sᶦḥw and Evolutionary Genesis: His praxis integrated indigenous agrarian knowledge, oral history, and spirit-defined heritage as tools for building national consciousness and epistemic freedom.

CHEIKH ANTA DIOP—*THE AFRICAN ORIGIN OF CIVILIZATION* (1974)

Paradigm Shifting: Diop overturned Eurocentric claims about the origins of civilization by demonstrating the African roots of ancient Egypt.

sᶦḥw r sᶦḥw and Evolutionary Genesis: His interdisciplinary methodology integrated historical linguistics, carbon dating, and cultural anthropology to reclaim African historical continuity and legitimacy.

CHINWEIZU—*THE WEST AND THE REST OF US* (1975)

Paradigm Shifting: Chinweizu exposed the epistemological violence of Euro-modernity and demanded a full decolonization of African thought and education.

sᶦḥw r sᶦḥw and Evolutionary Genesis: He mined indigenous African intellectual traditions to reconstruct decolonial frameworks rooted in sovereignty and cultural memory.

AYI KWEI ARMAH—*THE HEALERS* (1978)

Paradigm Shifting: Armah reframed healing and knowledge through African metaphysical sciences and collective well-being, opposing Western biomedical paradigms.

sᶦḥw r sᶦḥw and Evolutionary Genesis: He drew upon Dogon and Akan cosmology, positioning ancestral healing practices as valid epistemic methods and foundations for African unity.

MOLEFI KETE ASANTE—
AFROCENTRICITY (1980)

Paradigm Shifting: Asante formalized Afrocentricity, repositioning African people as agents of their own history, culture, and knowledge production.

s⁳ḥw r s⁳ḥw and Evolutionary Genesis: He reconstructed academic disciplines by drawing on Kemetian thought and African traditional wisdom, embedding identity, spirit, and culture into the center of inquiry.

ANGELA Y. DAVIS—*WOMEN, RACE &*
CLASS (1981)

Paradigm Shifting: Davis illuminated the interlocking nature of race, gender, and class, contributing to the framework of intersectionality and exposing the prison-industrial complex.

s⁳ḥw r s⁳ḥw and Evolutionary Genesis: She utilized Black liberation history, collective resistance memory, and ancestral feminist praxis as methodological tools for theory and organizing.

ALI A. MAZRUI—*THE AFRICANS: A*
TRIPLE HERITAGE (1986)

Paradigm Shifting: Mazrui proposed that African identity is formed by the interplay of indigenous, Islamic, and European influences, challenging reductionist cultural models.

s⁳ḥw r s⁳ḥw and Evolutionary Genesis: He traced African adaptability through the synthesis of diverse traditions, recovering epistemic pluralism within African civilization and resilience.

NGŨGĨ WA THIONG'O—*DECOLONISING*
THE MIND (1986)

Paradigm Shifting: Ngũgĩ argued that language is the battlefield of culture, and linguistic colonization was foundational to psychological and spirit-defined enslavement.

sꜣhw r sꜣhw and Evolutionary Genesis: He restored African languages as vessels of worldview and memory, establishing them as primary sites of philosophical inquiry and resistance.

PATRICIA HILL COLLINS—*BLACK FEMINIST THOUGHT* (1990)

Paradigm Shifting: Collins developed a Black feminist epistemology that prioritized lived experience, dialogue, and communal validation as forms of knowing.

sꜣhw r sꜣhw and Evolutionary Genesis: She used African American oral traditions, familial networks, and relational ethics as foundational frameworks for research and pedagogy.

JOHN HENRIK CLARKE—*AFRICANS AT THE CROSSROADS* (1991)

Paradigm Shifting: Clarke established African-centered historiography independent of Western validation, teaching that African people must write and interpret their own history.

sꜣhw r sꜣhw and Evolutionary Genesis: He grounded his scholarship in oral traditions, diaspora memory, and intergenerational knowledge transfer, rejecting Eurocentric linearity.

MAULANA KARENGA—*INTRODUCTION TO BLACK STUDIES* (1993)

Paradigm Shifting: Karenga reestablished African moral and philosophical principles, such as *Ma'at* and *Nguzo Saba*, as academic and social tools for Black Studies.

sꜣhw r sꜣhw and Evolutionary Genesis: He drew from ancient Kemetic ethical codes and Pan-African communal traditions to define educational standards and community development.

AMINA MAMA—BEYOND THE MASKS (1995)

Paradigm Shifting: Mama critiqued Euro-American feminism and advanced African feminist knowledge rooted in lived experience and indigenous understanding of gender.

sꜣḥw r sꜣḥw and Evolutionary Genesis: She recovered African gender cosmologies, social roles, and spirit-defined balance as foundations for African-centered feminist methodologies.

PAUL ZELEZA—MANUFACTURING AFRICAN STUDIES AND CRISES (1997)

Paradigm Shifting: Zeleza exposed the colonial structuring of African Studies as a discipline, challenging its academic boundaries and methodological bias.

sꜣḥw r sꜣḥw and Evolutionary Genesis: He used endogenous African categories, cultural memory, and historical continuity to map African identity and diasporic analysis.

SYLVIA WYNTER—UNSETTLING THE COLONIALITY OF BEING (2003)

Paradigm Shifting: Wynter dismantled the colonial invention of "Man" as the overrepresented figure of humanity, calling for a new definition of the human.

sꜣḥw r sꜣḥw and Evolutionary Genesis: She drew from African cosmology, Caribbean spirit-defined traditions, and decolonial poetics to generate new ontologies of being.

EDWIDGE DANTICAT—THE DEW BREAKER (2004)

Paradigm Shifting: Danticat challenged Western literary conventions by positioning trauma, exile, and intergenerational memory as central to diasporic narratives.

sꜣḥw r sꜣḥw and **Evolutionary Genesis:** She transformed Haitian oral history, cultural ritual, and ancestral voice into a narrative methodology of healing and survival.

WADE W. NOBLES—*SEEKING THE SAKHU* (2006)

Paradigm Shifting: Nobles dismantled Western psychological constructs by centering African metaphysics, spirit, and collective identity as foundations for wellness.

sꜣḥw r sꜣḥw and **Evolutionary Genesis:** He introduced the concepts of **Spirit(ness)** and **DEMM,** rooted in BaNtu cosmology, as methodological grounds for diagnosis, healing, and spirit-defined development.

CHAPTER 10

Summary

Synthesis, Implications for Africana Research

Throughout *sꜣḥw r sꜣḥw* and evolutionary genesis, the level of engagement was kept in (1) African affirmation that requires the acceptance of the idea of being spirit and Pan-African Humanism as defined by African deep thought and wisdom traditions and (2) decolonization of the mind that prohibits the elimination, distortion, or erasure of authentic African-centered thought ideations, theories, and interpretations.

This overall exposition has introduced *sꜣḥw r sꜣḥw* and evolutionary genesis as a new and unique methodology that reclaims, refines, and reactivates ancestral African knowledge systems to shape emergent theories, practices, and institutional formations for knowing and knowledge production. It centers *African genesis* not as a temporal past but as an *epistemic force*, fueling ontological reorientation. It aligns with *sꜣḥw r sꜣḥw* and evolutionary genesis as a research method for illuminating spirit. The paradigm of *sꜣḥw r sꜣḥw* and evolutionary genesis treats experience as *a living archive*, accessed through genetic memory, ritual knowledge, and spirit-defined consciousness. *sꜣḫw r sꜣḫw* and *sꜣḫw r sꜣḫw* and evolutionary genesis purports the ontological groundings of African Being with spirit(ness) being the condition of *being Spirit*, not as an essence that humans possess but as the primary, essential substance *from which* life is and emerges. Building on Skh, this exposition has also reintroduced DEMM being is the embodiment of divine energy materialized into physical form and functioning across visible and invisible realms.

These constructs affirm personhood, familyhood, and peoplehood through spirit-defined ontology, not Eurocentric categories of personality or pathology. Throughout this discussion, we recognize that traditional research designs often ignore African ontologies. *sꜣḫw r sꜣḫw* and evolutionary genesis reframe specifics like *sample selection* to include the visible realm for African-ascended people across the diaspora (Afro-Brazilian, Afro-Cuban, African Americans, Afro-Colombians, Afro-Brits, Afro-Australians, Francophone and Anglophone Africans) and the invisible realm of the ancestors, spirit guides, yet-to-be-born children, spirit-defined archetypes (e.g., Ogun, Nzambi, Nommo).

By utilizing *sꜣḫw r sꜣḫw* and evolutionary genesis, which necessitate integrating *Spirit(ness)*, DEMM, *BaNtu cosmology*, this book offers proposes a methodology for reclaiming research, healing, and governance as spirit-defined and a spirit-defined and spirit-driven process. The essential paradigm shifting repositions Africa and its diaspora, not as objects of knowing, but as *originators and custodians* of a cosmologically grounded science of being. Evolutionary genesis applies epistemological frames to methodological processes, and it is capable of serving as a conceptual roadmap for *Pan-African Studies* and *Africology* as well as a strategic foundation for global Black development, sovereignty, and governance.

sᵢḫw r sᵢḫw and evolutionary genesis are proposed as fluid and organic processes that require ongoing engagement with ancient African knowledge systems. By rescuing, reclaiming, refining, and generating new frameworks, this approach ensures the integrity and relevance of African epistemic traditions while allowing them to guide the creation of innovative concepts, constructs, and programs. The work of sᵢḫw r sᵢḫw and evolutionary genesis invites researchers to enter the spirit-defined and relational domains of inquiry, and to be transformed by the process itself. As spirit beings housed in physical containers, the research task is not simply to know but to *Be* in right relation to all that has been, is, and will be.

This contribution *Skh to Skh: Evolutionary Genesis as an African-Centered Research Method* humbly attempts to guide the ethical, political, and institutional direction of African-centered research that emphasizes coherence with spirit-defined nature. It asserts the profound idea that African-centered research must support a global Pan-African future of epistemic, philosophical, paradigmatic, and cultural independence where African people everywhere can share a visionary and victorious reclamation of an African way of being.

CHAPTER 11
Possible Next Steps

The *sᵉḥw r sᵉḥw* and evolutionary genesis paradigm shifting proposition from "human being" to "spirit being" reorients identity, purpose, and praxis from a Eurocentric material-based ontology to an African-centered cosmology rooted in spirit(ness), interconnectedness, and DEMM. In this paradigm, *to be* is not simply to exist biologically or socially, but to emanate spirit, to reflect cosmic purpose, and to act in alignment with ancestral wisdom and divine essence across all life domains. When spirit being is translated to DEMM is placed at the center of all life spaces, each domain becomes a spirit-defined portal. Rather than fragmenting spirit across functional areas, this epistemic vision demands we integrate, activate, and emanate our divinity in all that we do. To be spirit being is to be whole, connected, purpose-driven, and cosmically aligned. From education to economics, from family to futurism, each space can become a ritual field for spirit to walk, speak, and shine.

Being a spirit being means acting, knowing, building, loving, governing, and imagining as one who is DEMM—not bound by flesh, but expressive of spirit. Being a "spirit being" for the

African-centered research methodologist can be actualized within eight major life space areas, which, in turn, can serve as the arenas for Africana/Africologist research.

SOCIAL LIFE SPACE

Spirit being manifestation:

- Practices *Ubuntu*—"I am because we are"—honoring collective spirit over individual ego.
- Uses language and rituals (greetings, libations, proverbs) that affirm interbeing.
- Engages in communal joy, drumming, dance, and storytelling as spirit-affirming practices that restore balance in community relations.

Example: A community member mediating a conflict by invoking ancestors and restoring "right relations" through rituals of reconciliation and truth-telling.

FAMILY LIFE SPACE

Spirit being manifestation:

- Views the family not as a nuclear unit, but as an *ancestral continuum*—past, present, yet-to-be-born.
- Names children based on spirit-defined messages, dreams, or ancestor visitations.
- Practices **"Zaya discourse"**—ancestral memory transmission through imagination, dreams, and oral traditions.

Example: A grandmother teaches values not by rules but through proverbs and ancestral stories that encode moral wisdom and spirit-defined connectivity.

ECONOMIC LIFE SPACE

Spirit being manifestation:

- Creates economic practices that reflect *Ma'at* (balance, reciprocity) rather than extraction or greed.
- Engages in "sacred commerce," where trade honors ancestors and spirit-defined principles (e.g., giving thanks before exchange).
- Centers *Ubuntu economics*: economic activity that sustains the people, land, and spirit.

Example: A Black-owned cooperative that distributes profits to support wellness initiatives, ancestral rituals, and land stewardship.

EDUCATIONAL LIFE SPACE

Spirit being manifestation:

- Shifts education from memorizing content to *awakening spirit*, identity, purpose, and ancestral memory.
- Curriculum includes *Sankofa* (retrieval of ancestral knowledge), ritual learning, and spirit-defined cosmologies.
- Teachers are seen as *healers and spirit guides* rather than just information transmitters.

Example: A school where students start the day with libations, meditation, and ancestral invocation, and study African cosmologies as foundational science.

POLITICAL LIFE SPACE

Spirit being manifestation:

- Politics becomes the spirit-define dart of stewarding people's purpose and protection.
- Leadership is ancestralized (e.g., wise elders and diviners guide policy through spirit-informed insight).

- Laws are evaluated by their alignment with *Ma'at* and cosmic order, not just legality.

Example: Community council includes diviners, elders, and youth who co-govern using ancestral protocols and spirit-based consensus.

RELIGIOUS OR SPIRIT-DEFINED LIFE SPACE

Spirit being manifestation:

- Spirit-defined is not housed in institutions but is *an ontological state of being.*
- Engages with the *visible and invisible realms* as coexisting, reciprocal spaces.
- Worship involves *vibration (sound, rhythm, incantation), movement (dance, gesture), and offerings (libations, food, song)* to harmonize with spirit.

Example: A religious ceremony uses drumming to activate trance, allowing communication with ancestors and divine forces for healing.

ENTREPRENEURIAL LIFE SPACE

Spirit being manifestation:

- Entrepreneurship is seen as *a divine calling to serve*, not just to earn.
- Business ventures are **ancestrally rooted,** culturally affirming, and spirit-definedly protective.
- Enterprises integrate art, rhythm, ritual, and African symbols as part of daily function.

Example: A fashion designer uses Adinkra and Kemetic symbols not just for style but to awaken cultural pride and spirit-defined resonance in their clientele.

FUTURIST LIFE SPACE

Spirit being manifestation:

- Envisions the future through *ancestral technologies*, cosmological time (cyclical not linear), and *spirit-encoded memory*.
- Innovates from **"evolutionary genesis"**—retrieving ancient spirit-defined truths to inform future systems of governance, health, and learning.
- Engages **bio-phonic communication** and quantum entanglement concepts as evidence of ancestral presence in future making.

Example: A Pan-African futurist uses AI not to replace humanity but to encode ancestral ethics and spirit-defined rhythm into future technological interfaces.

Afterword

Toward a Service Treatment Praxis

SꜢḤW R SꜢḤW AND EVOLUTIONARY GENESIS

Western systems are often driven by compliance, data points, and externally imposed standards. The African-centered paradigm calls for a shift toward alignment with purpose, restoration of relational integrity, and emanation of spirit across realms (visible and invisible). This final step requires understanding that African-centered service is not a profession but a cosmic obligation. To provide serve to others is to ritually honor the Divine in others, to become a vessel through which ancestral light is remembered and projected. This is what it means to be cosmically aligned—to allow spirit to reenter our systems not as metaphor, but as method. To do this, we must commit to deep study, communal accountability, ritual literacy, and personal transformation.

An essential next treatment step therefore would be to accept the *sꜢḥw r sꜢḥw* and Evolutionary Genesis framework and abandon the illusion of fragmentation. We must no longer act as though spirit belongs only in temples or ceremonies. The clinic, the classroom, the courtroom, the home—each becomes a ritual container for DEMM to express, transform, and unify. In every service rendered, the question must become: How Is Spirit walking here? If not, we must realign our steps.

The proposition advanced by the $s^i\underline{h}w$ r $s^i\underline{h}w$ framework and the paradigm of evolutionary genesis invites a transformative departure from the prevailing Western view of "human being" toward an African-centered reorientation that understands the self as spirit being. This reorientation is not rhetorical; it is a call to action—a necessary epistemic, ontological, and practical shift that alters how we define identity, structure services, and evaluate purpose across all domains of life.

At the heart of this shift is the recognition that Being is not reducible to biology or behavior but is, in its truest form, the emanation of Spiritness—a living vibration of DEMM. The implications for service systems are profound. Spirit being must no longer be fragmented across functional areas, diminished in assessments, or excluded from the so-called evidence-based practice. Instead, it must be centered, activated, and honored as the ground of all being and becoming.

Accordingly, a next treatment step would be to reject frameworks that locate identity as dysfunction or pathology. Service models must instead affirm the client or participant as inherently whole, though possibly disoriented or disconnected due to generational harm or sociocultural misalignment. By embracing spirit being, we affirm the sacredness of life as a journey of cosmic intention. This reframing would require service providers to reimagine their role, not merely as fixers or helpers, as facilitators of remembrance, witnesses to spirit, and activators of ancestral purpose. This means accepting the challenge to move from pathology to purpose.

The $s^i\underline{h}w$ r $s^i\underline{h}w$ and Evolutionary Genesis framework would require reimagining our treatment spaces, for example, clinics, classrooms, courts, and community programs, as spirit-defined portals. Each domain becomes a ritual field, a stage for spiritual coherence and ancestral alignment. In this context, restoration (treatment) becomes a transmission of sacred memory; economic activity becomes a ritual of collective restoration; and the inter-connected rings of personhood, familyhood, and neighborhood family work becomes ancestral reweaving. These shifts invite practitioners to embed meaning, rhythm, and spirit-driven intention into every tool, interaction, and outcome. To center DEMM is to regard each life act as sacred expression. From intake forms to community planning meetings, spirit must be allowed to walk, speak, and shine. Programs must create conditions for spirit to emerge, not just metrics to control outcomes. This demands humility, cosmological literacy, and ancestral accountability from all practitioners. Treatment, intervention, and service models must all evolve to reflect this spirit-defined ontology.

Abner Boles, III

Program Director and Board President

African American Healing Alliance

Chief Executive Officer

Business Solutions Design and development group

Appendix

Conducting Evolutionary Genesis

A STEP-BY-STEP PROCEDURE

The following is a proposed step-by-step procedure for research methodologist implementing the concept of *sꜣḥw r sꜣḥw* and evolutionary genesis as a knowledge acquisition and development process. Designed for researchers, educators, program designers, and clinicians, this approach is grounded in rescuing, reclaiming, and refining African epistemic traditions to guide contemporary practice and thought. Each step ensures fidelity to African worldviews while allowing for organic evolution and application in modern contexts.

STEP 1: CLARIFY THE FOCUS AREA

Objective: Identify the specific domain or focus area (e.g., education, mental health, philosophy, program design) where the *sꜣḥw r sꜣḥw* and evolutionary genesis process will be applied.

1. **Define the problem or objective**—What issue, question, or area requires deeper illumination/understanding and development from an African-centered perspective?

   - Example: The need for culturally congruent mental health services for African-ascendent populations.

2. Identify the scope—Are you looking at broad cultural frameworks or specific intellectual traditions (e.g., Yoruba cosmology, Kongo metaphysics)?

   • Example: Focusing on Kongo cosmology to develop a community healing program.

3. Clarify expected outcomes—What is the goal of applying *evolutionary genesis*? New programs, theoretical models, curricula, or service delivery methods?

   • EXAMPLE: Developing a culturally grounded spirit-defined and spirit-driven interventions.

STEP 2: RESCUE ANCIENT KNOWLEDGE AND THOUGHT

Objective: Recover ancient African intellectual traditions and worldviews relevant to the identified focus area.

1. **Research foundational African knowledge**—Begin with an extensive literature review of the relevant African cultures, intellectual traditions, and epistemologies.

   • Use works by scholars such as Cheikh Anta Diop, Wade Nobles, Kobi Kambon, and Marimba Ani.

   • Example: Investigating the concept of *Ma'at* in Kemetic philosophy as it relates to social harmony.

2. **Document oral traditions**—Interview or collaborate with African elders, healers, and traditional knowledge bearers to capture oral histories and practices.

   • Example: Recording the teachings of a Yoruba *babalawo* on the cosmological understanding of health and balance.

3. **Catalog findings**—Organize the information collected from both literature and oral traditions into thematic areas, ensuring that these remain faithful to their original cultural meanings.

STEP 3: RECLAIM KNOWLEDGE AND REFRAME IT FOR CONTEMPORARY USE

Objective: Assert ownership of the rescued knowledge and position it within a modern framework while ensuring cultural fidelity.

1. **Contextualize the knowledge**—Reclaim the knowledge as authentic African wisdom by refuting distortions or misrepresentations introduced through colonial and Western frameworks.

   • Example: Correct the reduction in African cosmologies to mere folklore by emphasizing their philosophical depth and relevance in healing practices.

2. **Reframe knowledge for contemporary issues**—Translate the knowledge into applicable frameworks for modern challenges. Maintain fidelity to the epistemic core but allow for flexibility in its application.

   • Example: Utilize the principles of *Ma'at* to create a community-based conflict resolution program.

3. **Develop languaging and terminology**—Languaging connotes action. It gives the noun language, "vitalism," and manifests as a living word. Language, and the knowing (action) it represents, reflects and represents a people's cultural verve (spirit). Languaging is the process of using language as a tool for constructing reality and shaping consciousness. Languaging and consistent terminology involves the intentional use of language to reflect and reinforce African cultural values, perspectives, and worldviews. Languaging is a powerful means of reclaiming narratives and redefining identities in ways that honor the lived experiences of African-ascendent people.

   • In service delivery, languaging accomplishes the crucial task of making the invisible visible and meaning-making

   • Example: Introducing the concept of "*Ubuntu*" in organizational leadership practices to emphasize communal responsibility.

- In research methods, languaging guarantees the authenticity and integrity of the process.

STEP 4: REFINE KNOWLEDGE THROUGH CRITICAL REFLECTION AND ADAPTATION

Objective: Adapt the reclaimed knowledge to the specific modern context while maintaining its genetic authenticity and integrity.

1. Test the knowledge in real-world settings—Implement small-scale pilot programs or theoretical applications to evaluate how the rescued and reclaimed knowledge interacts with current systems.

   - Example: Introduce a pilot restorative wellness program based on Kongo cosmology, assessing its effectiveness in urban communities.

2. Evaluate feedback and outcomes—Use feedback from participants, stakeholders, and experts to assess the alignment of the adapted knowledge with both cultural fidelity and practical relevance.

   - Example: Collect feedback from Bwana Mbotis on how integrating African spirit-defined practices affects therapeutic outcomes.

3. Refine through iteration—Adjust the application of knowledge based on critical feedback, ensuring that it evolves while still rooted in its authentic tradition.

   - Example: Modify the restorative program by incorporating additional rituals or practices that were initially overlooked but proved beneficial during the pilot phase.

STEP 5: GENERATE NEW CONSTRUCTS, METHODS, AND PROGRAMS

Objective: Create innovative frameworks, programs, and practices that are guided by the evolutionary process of ancient African thought and epistemology.

1. Design new programs or services—Based on the refinement process, develop programs, methods, or theories that integrate the ancient knowledge into contemporary frameworks.

   • Example: Create a culturally rooted curriculum that uses Kongo cosmology as the foundation for conflict resolution in schools.

2. Develop theoretical models—Build models that can explain modern phenomena through the lens of reclaimed African traditions, contributing to the development of African-centered theoretical frameworks.

   • Example: Develop a new model of well-being based on Dogon metaphysics, integrating concepts of spirit, matter, and community.

3. Create research assessment tools—Design culturally congruent tools, assessment models, or guides that support the application of African knowledge systems in various professional fields.

   • Example: Develop a practitioner's guide for researchers that includes African-centered classificatory tools and restorative techniques.

STEP 6: ENSURE ORGANIC DEVELOPMENT AND CONTINUOUS REFLECTION

Objective: Sustain the process of knowledge evolution through continuous reflection, feedback, and adaptation, ensuring the ongoing relevance of ancient knowledge in modern contexts.

1. Establish feedback mechanisms—Create channels for ongoing reflection and feedback to ensure the applied knowledge remains dynamic and responsive to evolving contexts.

   • Example: Hold regular community forums or professional roundtables to evaluate the impact of newly implemented programs.

2. Revisit and refine periodically—Periodically revisit the foundational knowledge and adapt the applied frameworks as new challenges or opportunities emerge.

   • Example: Every few years, reevaluate the restorative program's alignment with both ancient African practices and modern social needs.

3. Document the ongoing process—Keep detailed records of each iteration of refinement and development, allowing future generations to continue the *sꜣḥw r sꜣḥw* and evolutionary genesis process.

   • Example: Create case studies or reflective journals documenting how African epistemologies have shaped successful interventions in education or mental health.

STEP 7: GUARDING AGAINST DEFAULTING

Objective: Recognize that without intentionally giving primacy to the science of African human functioning one will automatically revert to Western (Euro-American) psychology by "default."

The danger of default is evidenced by presumptions of the universality of Western (Euro-American) worldview or more dangerously making assumptions of cultural or value equivalence between African Americans and Euro-Americans. When in the state of default practitioners can become what amounts to being perpetrators and/or collaborators of clinical assault and/or malpractice.

SꜢḤW R SꜢḤW 𓂀𓏤 ⎯ 𓂀𓏤

The misnomer *Hieroglyph* is a Greek word meaning *"sacred carving"* (from *hieros* = sacred, *glypho* = carve). The ancient Kemites viewed writing as a spirit-driven technology, not simply a tool for communication. Each glyph carried both phonetic sound and spirit power, functioning as a portal between the visible and invisible realms. *Medu Netcher* is the indigenous accurate African name, emphasizing sacred speech rather than carved symbols. *Medu Netcher* means Sacred Divine Speech, the living language of spirit that the Kemites believed was given by the divine to order reality. In the Medu Netcher, **sꜣḫw** (𓂀𓏤) refers to a spirit-defined awakened or "transfigured" being. It is both a noun and a verb. It is both a *state of being* and *process of becoming*. In actuality, the term sꜣḫw (𓂀𓏤) for the ancient Kemites carries layered meanings: illumination, realization, and spirit-driven effectiveness. It describes the condition of being "made effective" (*akh*), a state where the knowing spirit is not only conscious but empowered in both the visible and invisible realms. sꜣḫw (𓂀𓏤) *is not a body of knowledge to be consumed but a process of Being to be lived.* In both ancient and modern African thought, knowledge is **ontological** (a way of being), not merely epistemological. As an Illumination, it is cumulative and spiraling, not linear. Spirit is self-referential and expansive, always illuminating itself.

The Medu Netcher, in the title, represents the Kemetic expression, **sꜣḫw r sꜣḫw** (𓂀𓏤 ⎯ 𓂀𓏤), that translates as "to cause to become sꜣḫw for the sake of becoming sꜣḫw." It signifies an unfolding process of transforming into one who is spirit-defined awakening or spirit-driven luminosity. This ancient concept conveys a recursive, initiatory process of becoming as "becoming the one who becomes." The connective r (⎯)—meaning "to," "toward," "for," or "in relation to"—creates a dynamic relationship between the two instances of **sꜣḫw**. This grammatical construction is more than linear connection; it describes a movement of being into itself. It is not "illumination *and* illumination," but illumination toward illumination. It is not two static states, but a processual unfolding of deeper knowing. This recursive pattern is common in African spirit-defined discourse, where repetition and reflexivity are strategies of intensification. The second term does not simply mirror the first. It expands, deepens, and transforms it. The transliteration and meaning of this term are **sꜣḫw** (illumination, realization, spiritual effectiveness, enlightenment), **r** (to, toward, in relation to), and **sꜣḫw** (illumination again, reflexive repetition.

When doubled through the phrase **sꜣḫw r sꜣḫw**, the concept signals recursive illumination, a process where knowledge and spirit-driven realization are not static but unfold into greater and greater depths of being. This reflects a self-reflexive epistemology where illumination leads to illumination, realization deepens realization, and spirit amplifies spirit. Hence, **sꜣḫw r sꜣḫw** (𓊰𓏤 ‒ 𓊰𓏤) means "Illumination toward Illumination," or "Realization into Realization."

The phrase **sꜣḫw r sꜣḫw** encapsulates a core African principle where **Being is not fixed but generative.** The title phrase expresses "recursive deepening of enlightenment," a process of *being becoming more effective in spirit.* **sꜣḫw r sꜣḫw** (𓊰𓏤 ‒ 𓊰𓏤) and **Evolutionary Genesis** therein mean that African-centered research methodology should represent and reflect the sacred path of becoming; the illuminating the illumined; and the reclamation of African knowing. This aligns with the Kemetic ideal of eternal becoming (*nfr*) and sacred continuity. This glyph captures both the cosmological and epistemological rhythm of life understood as a spiraling journey of return, refinement, and illumination.

Accordingly, and as implied in the title, African-centered research must move beyond surface knowledge to embrace ontological illumination with knowing as being and knowledge as energy made manifest.

References

Abimbola, W. (1976). *Ifá: An exposition of Ifá literary corpus*. Oxford University Press.

Akbar, N. (2004). *Akbar papers in African psychology*. Mind Productions.

Armah, A. K. (1973) *Two thousand seasons*. East African Publishing House.

Armah, A. K. (1978). *The healers*. East African Publishing House.

Asante, M. K. (1980). *Afrocentricity: The theory of social change*. Amulefi Publishing Company.

Bynum, E. B. (2012). *The African unconscious: Roots of ancient mysticism and modern psychology*. Inner Traditions.

Carruthers, J. H. (1999). *Intellectual warfare*. Third World Press.

Clarke, J. H. (1991). *Africans at the Crossroads: Notes for an African World Revolution* (xv + 450 pp.). Africa World Press.

Collins, P. H. (1990). *Black feminist thought: Knowledge, consciousness, and the politics of empowerment*. Unwin Hyman.

Danticat, E. (2004). *The Dew breaker*. Alfred A. Knopf.

Davis, A. Y. (1983). *Women, race & class*. Vintage Books.

Diop, C. A. (1974). *The African origin of civilization: Myth or reality* (M. Cook, Trans Ed.). Lawrence Hill Books.

Chinweizu. (1975). The west and the rest of us.

Diouf, S. A. (1998). *Servants of Allah: African Muslims enslaved in the Americas*. NYU Press.

Du Bois, W. E. B. (1903). *The souls of Black folk: Essays and sketches*. A. C. McClurg & Co.

Ehret, C. I. (2001). *A historical-comparative reconstruction of Nilo-Saharan*. Rüdiger Köppe Verlag,

Fanon, F. (1967). *Black skin, white masks.* Grove Press.

Fu-Kiau, K. K. B. (1991). *Self-healing power and therapy: Old teachings from Africa.* Vantage Press.

Fu-Kiau, K. K. B. (2001). *African cosmology of the Bantu-Kongo: Principles of life & living.* Athelia Henrietta Press.

Greene, S. E. (2002). *Spirit-defined sites and the colonial encounter: A history of meaning and memory in Ghana.* Indiana University Press.

Griaule, M. (1965). *Conversations with Ogotemmêli: An introduction to Dogon religious ideas.* Oxford University Press.

Gyekye, K. (1995). *An essay on African philosophical thought: The Akan conceptual scheme.* Temple University Press.

Janzen, J. M. (1982). *Lemba, 1650–1930: A drum of affliction in Africa and the New World* (p. 57). Garland.

Kagame, A. (1976). *La philosophie bantu-rwandaise de l'Être* (p. 23). Présence Africaine.

Kambon, K. (1998). *African/Black psychology in the American context: An African-centered approach.* Nubian Nation Publications.

Karenga, M. (1993). *Introduction to Black Studies.* University of Sankore Press.

Mama, A. (1995). *Beyond the masks: race, gender and subjectivity.* Routledge Psychology Press.

Mazrui, A. A. (1986). *The Africans: A triple heritage.*

Mbiti, J. S. (1969). *African religions & philosophy.* Heinemann.

Thiong'o, N. (1986). *Decolonising the mind: The politics of language in African literature.* James Currey.

Ngubane, J. K. (1979). *Conflict of minds.* Books in Focus.

Nkrumah, K. (1964). *Consciencism: Philosophy and ideology for decolonization and development with reference to the African revolution.* Heinemann.

Nobles, W. W. (1978). The archeology of the African spirit: Toward a deeper discourse. *Black Studies Journal of Black Studies.*

Nobles, W. W. (Ed.). (2006). *Seeking the Sakhu: Foundational writings for an African psychology* (Vol. 77). Third World Press.

Nobles, W. W. (2015a). Cultural resistance to psychic terrorism. In M. J. Shujaa & K. J. Shujaa (Eds.), *Encyclopedia of African cultural heritage in North America.* Sage.

Nobles, W. W. (2015b). *The island of memes: Haiti's unfinished revolution*. Black Classical Press.

Nobles, W. W. (2023). *SKH: From Black psychology to the science of being*. Universal Write Publications, LLC.

Obenga, T. (2004). *African Philosophy: The Pharaonic Period, 2780–330 B.C.* Popenguine, Senegal: Per Ankh.

Oladipo, O. (1992). The idea of African philosophy (p. 48). Brill.

Somé, M. P. (1998). *The healing wisdom of Africa* (pp. 101–105). Tarcher/Putnam.

Tempels, P., Rubbens, A., & King, C. (1959). *Bantu philosophy* (p. 127). Présence Africaine.

Théophile, O. (2004). *Egypt: Ancient History of African Philosophy*. In K. Wiredu (Eds.), *A Companion to African philosophy* (pp. 29–49). Wiley-Blackwell.

Viriri, A., & Mungwini, P. (2010). *African cosmology and the duality of western Hegemony: The search for an African identity*. Institute of Pan African Studies.

Wynter, S. (2003). Unsettling the coloniality of being/power/truth/freedom: Towards the human, after man, its overrepresentation—An argument. *CR: The New Centennial Review, 3*(3), 257–337. https://doi.org/10.1353/ncr.2004.0015

Zeleza, P. T. (1997). *Manufacturing African studies and crises*. CODESRIA Books.

About the Author

Baba Dr Wade Ifágbemì Sàngódáre Nobles

Dr Wade W. Nobles is the son of Annie Mae Cotton (1914b) and John Nobles (1900b). John Nobles' father was Mims Nobles who was born into the barbarism of American slavery in 1863. Mims' father was Wade Nobles who was born into the savagery of slavery in 1836. Wade Nobles was the oldest son of Candace/Agnes (Cilla) who was also born into captivity in Edgefield, South Carolina, in 1810. Dr Nobles is the namesake of his great grandfather, Agnes' oldest son. His mother and father named him Wade, which means one who is able to tread through difficult matter like slavery, mud, snow, or ignorance. Dr Nobles is a Co-Founder and Past President, The ABPsi; Chairperson, ABPsi Pan African Black Psychology Global Initiative; Founder, Professor Emeritus, Black Psychology and Africana Studies, SFSU, recipient of an Honorary Doctor of Humane Letters, CSUDH and the founding Executive Director (retired) of the Institute for the Advanced Study of Black Family Life and Culture (est 1968) in Oakland where he spent over 40 years researching, documenting, publishing, designing and implementing African-centered service and training programs. Dr Nobles has studied classical African philosophy (Kemet, Twa, and Nubian) and traditional African wisdom traditions (Akan, Yoruba, Bantu, Wolof, Dogon, Fon, Lebou, etc.) as the grounding for the development of an authentic Black psychology. His professional career and life's work has been no less than a formal engagement in the ongoing theoretical development and programmatic application of African (Black) psychology, African-centered thought, and cultural grounding to address the liberation and restoration of the African mind and world-wide development of African people. He has conducted eighty nationally funded community-based research, training and development projects. Dr Nobles initiated the IFA spiritual system of Nigeria in 1992 and named Ifágbemì Sàngódáre. An internationally recognized Pan Africanist, Dr Nobles is the author of over one hundred articles, chapters, research reports, and books; the coauthor of the seminal article in Black Psychology, Voodoo or IQ: An Introduction to African Psychology; the author of *African Psychology: Toward its Reclamation, Reascension and Revitalization*; *Seeking the Sakhu: Foundational Writings in African Psychology*, an anthology of over thirty years of African-centered research and scholarship, *The Island of Memes: Haiti's Unfinished Revolution* described by Dr Theophile Obenga as perhaps the most important book of the last five decades, and his recent contribution, *SKH, From Black Psychology to the Science of Being*, traces the advent of Black psychology and its evolution to the science of being. His work has been translated into Spanish, Portuguese, and French. Baba Dr Nobles has served as a visiting professor in Salvador de Bahia and Sao Paulo in Brazil, England, Ghana, West Africa, and Cape Town, South Africa. He currently serves as the chairperson of the ABPsi Pan African Black Psychology Global Initiative with members in Brazil, South Africa, Nigeria, Great Britain, Jamaica, Canada, Haiti, and Ghana. He served as the lead author of the African American Wellness Hub Complex Design Report (2017), for the Behavioral

Health Care Services in Alameda County California, and is the project director for the Interim Virtual Hub Project.

SIGNIFICANT BLACK PSYCHOLOGY LITERARY CONTRIBUTIONS

- *Voodoo or IQ: An Introduction to African Psychology*
- *African Psychology: Toward its Reclamation, Reascension and Revitalization*
- *Seeking the Sakhu: Foundational Writings in African Psychology*, an anthology
- *The Island of Memes: Haiti's Unfinished Revolution*
- *Skh: From Black Psychology to The Science of Being*

SPECIAL JOURNALS

- Co-editor *Afrikan-centered Psychology: Illuminating the Human Spirit, South African Journal*—Alternation Special Edition
- Pan African Discussion of African Psychology, *Journal of Black Psychology*, Vol. 39(3); 2013
- *Pan African humanness and sakhu djaer as praxis for indigenous knowledge systems.* Alternation Special Edition, 18, 36–59; 2016.

Postscript

This manuscript represents a major contribution to African-centered research methodology that could only have emerged from the profound scholarly vision and creativity of Baba Dr Wade Ifágbemì Sàngódáre Nobles. The work perfectly embodies the series' mission of advancing accessible, practical research methods while maintaining deep theoretical sophistication and spiritual grounding. One thing that distinguishes this text is its revolutionary repositioning of *research purpose* beyond mere knowledge acquisition to encompass the spiritual and transformative dimensions of inquiry. Dr Nobles' conceptualization of spirit as the heart of research fundamentally transforms how we understand the research enterprise, moving it from researcher-centered mechanistic data collection to a sacred practice of discovery and connection. This paradigm shift offers researchers a more holistic and culturally grounded approach to understanding human experience.

The manuscript's structural design, which closes with clear procedural steps, provides readers with concrete pathways for putting to practice these profound methodological insights. The systematic presentation of key components of an African paradigm, coupled with the innovative *Zaya discourse approach*, creates a new way of seeing and a comprehensive framework that is both theoretically rigorous and practically applicable. The *call-and-response approach* to hypothesis testing represents a particularly creative methodological innovation that honors

African oral traditions while maintaining scientific validity. Throughout the text, Dr Nobles provides the discipline with new language through specialized spiritual concepts. Terms like *"multiple realms"* are illuminated through examples such as dreams, rituals, behavior, and spoken words, ensuring that readers can grasp both the theoretical significance and practical applications of these concepts. The work's emphasis on engaging *"the fullness of what is real"* challenges conventional research boundaries and invites scholars to embrace a more expansive understanding of reality that includes spiritual, cultural, and experiential dimensions often marginalized in western traditions of research. This Ubuntu methodological approach represents a significant advancement in African-centered research practices.

Like any transformational text, this one will undoubtedly require multiple readings to fully appreciate its depth and complexity, a testament to the richness of thought and the transformative potential of the methodological framework and new conceptual language presented. Dr Nobles has created not just a research manual, but a philosophical and spiritual guide to inquiry that will reshape how researchers approach the study of the people of the African world. The manuscript stands as an essential contribution to Africana Studies. It is a text that only Dr Nobles' unique combination of scholarly expertise, creativity, spiritual wisdom, and methodological innovation could have produced. It represents a vital addition to African-centered research literature and will serve as an indispensable resource for scholars seeking to conduct research that honors both rigorous methodology and cultural alignment.

Dr Serie McDougal, III

Series Editor

The Little Black Book Series

Research Methodology, Theory and Praxis

S3ḤW R S3ḤW (𓇌𓃭𓏤 ⸺ 𓇌𓃭𓏤)

Is defined as African-centered research methodology. It should represent and reflect the sacred path of becoming, illuminating the illumined, and the reclamation of African knowing.

Index